This book belongs to:

Amelia

It was given to me by:

HOΣtN

On:

rɛrɛr

Bedtime BIBLE Stories

More Than 180 Faith-Building Readings

Bedtime BIBLE Stories

Jane Landreth
Daniel Partner
Renae Brumbaugh
Linda Carlblom

BARBOUR BOOKS
An Imprint of Barbour Publishing, Inc.

Member of the
Evangelical Christian
Publishers Association

Printed in the United States of America.
04771 0914 UG

Welcome to the Wonderful World of Bible Stories!

The Bible is a big book, filled with fascinating people, places, and events. And this book—*Bedtime Bible Stories*—explains those people, places, and events in ways that children ages five to eight can easily understand.

Here are more than 180 carefully retold Bible stories presented in biblical order—from God's creation of the world in Genesis 1 to His renewal of heaven and earth in Revelation 22. Each story is keyed to a memorable passage of scripture, and takes your kids beyond the story itself. They'll be challenged to consider how those Bible stories relate to their lives today.

Packed with colorful illustrations and thoughtful "prayer starters," *Bedtime Bible Stories* is the perfect book to bring you and your kids together for some spiritual quality time. Enjoy!

"In the Beginning God. . ."

In the beginning God created the heavens and the earth.

GENESIS 1:1 NLT

When you read a book, it is important to know what that book is about. This is not hard to do. Sometimes the name of the book tells you. The book called *The Cat in the Hat* is about a cat wearing a hat. There is a book called *The Adventures of Peter Rabbit*. It is a book about exciting things that happen to a rabbit named Peter. And the name *The Cat in the Hat Comes Back* tells you just what that book is about.

What do you think the Bible is about? The word *bible* means "book." That name doesn't give a hint about what's inside the book. But read the first four words of the Bible: "In the beginning God. . ." Do these words tell you what the Bible is about? Yes! The Bible is about God.

True, the Bible tells about many things and many people. But all in all, the Bible is meant to show you who God is and what God has done for you.

Dear God,

thank You for the Bible, which tells me all about You.

"Let Bright Lights Appear."

And God said, "Let bright lights appear in the sky."
GENESIS 1:14 NLT

It is good that the sky is not empty. How boring that would be! All day long, we would see only blue sky. And at night, we would see nothing but black. God wanted more than this. So the Bible says, "God made two great lights, the sun and the moon, to shine down upon the earth. The greater one, the sun, presides during the day; the lesser one, the moon, presides through the night. He also made the stars."

The greater light rules the day. What is that light? It is the sun. The lesser light rules the night. What do you think this is? That's easy! It is the moon. And God made the stars, too.

On the first day there was light. But God wanted more than just that light. So He made the sun and moon and stars on the fourth day. You may be able to think of some reasons for these lights in the sky. They're very pretty, aren't they? The sunshine is so warm, and it makes things grow.

The Bible gives reasons for the sun, moon, and stars. It says that the sun divides the day from the night. The changing shape of the moon and patterns of the stars are sometimes helpful, kind of like road signs. And all three mark the changing seasons, days, and years. God said this was good. Don't you think so, too?

Dear God,

thank You for the sun, the moon, and the stars.

God Created the Animals

So God made the wild animals, the tame animals,
and all the small crawling animals to produce more
of their own kind. God saw that this was good.

GENESIS 1:25 NCV

Our wonderful God made all kinds of creatures, each one of a different shape, color, size, and attitude! God created the animals to live in the water and in the air first. Next He created the animals to live on the land. Then He made Adam, the first man, to take care of them all. And it only took God two days to make all those things. Wow! What an awesome Creator!

God made the giant forty-foot-tall dinosaurs and the tiny insect that was only the size of a pinhead. He gave animals eight legs, six legs, four legs, or two legs, and some no legs at all. Some animals had arms and some did not. Some animals had long necks and some short necks. Some had no necks. Some animals had fur, some had scales, some had feathers, and some had smooth skin. God made animals fat, skinny, tall, and short.

God made animals to live on the ground and some to live in trees. He made some animals to live on the tall mountains, some to live under the ground, some to fly in the sky, and some to swim in the deepest oceans. God created humans, too, each one different from the other. And it was all good. Wow! What a great God!

Dear God,

thank You for making so many different kinds of creatures, including me! It's wonderful that we are not all the same. Amen.

"So God Created. . ."

So God created great sea creatures and every sort
of fish and every kind of bird. . . . God made all sorts
of wild animals, livestock, and small animals.

GENESIS 1:21, 25 NLT

Do you like animals? If you answered yes, that's great! Because on the fifth day, God made the waters swarm with fish and other life. And the skies were filled with birds of every kind. God created big sea creatures, too. Think about all the different kinds of birds and fish there are. God made each one! God saw that this was good and blessed them all.

Wait, there's more!

The next day, God decided that there should be all kinds of other animals. So God made livestock like cattle, sheep, and goats. He made small animals and other wildlife. Plus, He made all the things that creep on the ground, like bugs and snakes and lizards.

Just about everything was made by this time, right? There was earth and sky and sea. The sun, moon, and stars were shining bright. Plants and trees and grass grew fresh and green. And there were animals everywhere, on land and in the sea and sky.

Could anything be missing? Think about it. . . . Yes, something is missing. You aren't there! There are no people yet. That's coming up next!

Dear God,

I love the animals
that You made—
thank You for
all of them!

"...and There He Placed the Man."

Then the Lord God planted a garden in Eden, in the east,
and there he placed the man he had created.

GENESIS 2:8 NLT

The first people God created were named Adam and Eve. They lived in a garden in Eden. This was a huge place. All the animals were there; trees and plants were growing; and rivers were flowing. Gold and precious stones were there. It must have been more beautiful than anything we've ever seen!

There God brought the animals and birds to the first man. Adam gave them all names. Imagine that! Adam was so smart that he could give a different name to every animal. He knew each and every one. Adam cared for the garden by working as a farmer. And it was there in the garden that God made the woman, Eve. The two were married in the garden at Eden.

If you like animals, you would have liked that garden. If you like flowers and trees, Eden was the place for you. What would you do there? You could swim in the rivers. You could collect precious stones. You could climb trees. You could plant and grow things. You could live with the animals.

All these things are wonderful. But they are not what really made Eden so wonderful. Here is why Eden was so good: God walked there in the cool evenings. He spoke to Adam and Eve, and they talked to Him. God was there, so it was paradise!

Dear God,
thank You
for our planet,
but most of all
for Your presence.

"Adam Chose a Name for Each One."

So the Lord God formed from the soil every kind of animal
and bird. He brought them to Adam to see what he would
call them, and Adam chose a name for each one.

Genesis 2:19 NLT

Do you know someone who you think is smart? This could be your mother or father, or a family member. Certainly, your schoolteacher knows a lot more than you do. But Adam was very smart. God brought all the animals to him. Then Adam chose a name for each one. Think of the names of as many animals as you can. How many animal names do you know? How many animal names does your father or mother know? How about your teacher?

Adam didn't just know every animal name, he is the one who gave all the animals their names! This means that he named every farm animal, every bird, and every wild animal. Adam probably named all the bugs and fish, too. This shows that God made people to be very, very smart!

Dear God,

thank You
for making
me so smart!

"I Will Make a Companion."

And the Lord God said, "It is not good for the man to be alone.
I will make a companion who will help him."
GENESIS 2:18 NLT

The very first man was all alone in that great big garden. God knew this, and He cared that Adam was alone. So God made all the animals and brought them to Adam. Was this how God wanted to fill Adam's loneliness? Were the animals to be Adam's companions on this earth?

Adam must have looked at each animal very carefully. After all, he gave each one a name. Giraffe, pig, alligator, dog, cat, elephant. How many kinds of animals are there? Tens of thousands, maybe millions. Adam knew them all. But after he had given them each a name, he was still alone. Adam still did not have a wife, someone to be his friend and helper in life.

There were so many wonderful animals. Adam must have enjoyed them. But no animal was right to be Adam's lifelong mate. What would you do to keep Adam from being alone? God did one final thing in order to complete the Creation. God made a woman.

Dear God,
thank You for making
a helper for Adam.

"God Made a Woman."

So the Lord God caused Adam to fall into a deep sleep.
He took one of Adam's ribs. . . . Then the Lord God made
a woman from the rib and brought her to Adam.

Think of all that God did to make the heavens and the earth. When God spoke the word, there was light and day and night, the sky and the dry land and the sea. When God spoke, the sun, moon, and stars appeared in the sky. Over and over again Genesis tells us, "And God said." That's how the Creation appeared—grass, herbs, and trees; fish and birds and even huge whales. All this happened because God spoke!

Then God changed the way of Creation. "And the Lord God formed a man's body from the dust of the ground and breathed into it the breath of life. And the man became a living person." God didn't just speak to make Adam. God worked to form him from dust. Then, so that Adam would have life, God breathed into him.

But Adam could not be alone. He needed a mate, someone who matched him in every way. This is why God made woman in a new and different way. God didn't speak or use dust, like before. Unlike everything else, woman was made from a part of Adam. And Adam said, "She is part of my own flesh and bone! She will be called 'woman,' because she was taken out of a man."

Dear God,

thank You for giving the breath of life to Adam— and to me!

"God Rested."

On the seventh day, having finished his task,
God rested from all his work.

GENESIS 2:2 NLT

The Bible tells about God's power. And God is strong, too. But God is much more than powerful and strong. God is also holy, eternal, faithful, wise, true, and good. God is light. God is love. God is so much that there are not enough words to tell it all!

The Bible is the book that tells us all we need to know about God. The first thing it says is that God is the Creator, and it tells the story of Creation. And there are not just six days in the Creation story. It took God seven days to finish making everything. The first six days were for working. Then on the seventh day, God rested from all His work.

First, God worked to create everything. What is the second thing the Bible tells about God? It says that God rested. But God is so strong and powerful. Why would He need to rest? Maybe to help us remember that we should take time to rest, too!

Dear God,

thank You for being who You are— powerful, holy, and full of love.

"...He Asked the Woman."

Now the serpent was the shrewdest of all the creatures the Lord God had made. "Really?" he asked the woman. "Did God really say you must not eat any of the fruit in the garden?"

GENESIS 3:1 NLT

The Bible is full of stories. Many of these are about good people who do good things. Bible stories tell of brave men and women and of people with courage and love. The Bible also tells stories of what God has done and will do for us.

But the Bible tells some sad stories, too. The saddest story tells how Adam and Eve failed God. It shows them leaving the wonderful Garden of Eden. We see them here for the first time living without God. This is the worst thing that could happen to them and to us.

There were many different kinds of trees in the garden. God said that the man and woman could eat the fruit of all those trees except for one—the Tree of the Knowledge of Good and Evil. This seems simple, doesn't it? But a powerful enemy of God entered Eden looking like a snake. This snake asked Eve which trees she could eat fruit from. It was a simple question, and Eve knew the right answer. But the snake tempted Eve to eat the forbidden fruit anyway, and this was the beginning of the fall of humanity into sin. Soon our simple, beautiful life with God would end.

Dear God,

help me to do what makes You happy— help me to do what is right.

"She Ate Some of the Fruit."

So she ate some of the fruit. She also gave some to her
husband, who was with her. Then he ate it, too.

GENESIS 3:6 NLT

A terrible thing happened when Adam and Eve ate the fruit of the only tree that God told them not to eat from. The people of the Garden of Eden died! God said this would happen if they ate of that tree. And it did happen.

It may not seem to you that they died. After all, they didn't drop dead after eating the fruit. Since this is true, it teaches that there are two kinds of death. One comes when our body dies. When our body is dead, we cannot live in this world anymore. But this is not what happened to Adam and Eve. After they ate the fruit, they knew their bodies were naked, and so they made clothes out of leaves. So we know they were still alive in their bodies.

But there is another kind of death.

Think of pretty flowers in a vase. They have all their color, and they may even smell good. They seem to be alive, but they are not. These flowers have been cut off from their roots in the soil. They can't get their food from the earth anymore. In time, they will wilt away. In fact, they are already dead.

In the same way, Adam and Eve were cut off from God. That's what God meant when He said they would die if they ate the forbidden fruit.

Dear God

teach me to be
alive in You—
to trust
what You say.

"...the Tree of Life."

After banishing them from the garden, the Lord God stationed mighty angelic beings to the east of Eden. And a flaming sword flashed back and forth, guarding the way to the tree of life.

GENESIS 3:24 NLT

There was another important tree in the Garden of Eden. To understand the Bible, you must know about this tree. It is the Tree of Life.

Adam and Eve could have chosen to eat from the tree of life. Instead, they ate from the Tree of the Knowledge of Good and Evil. So they died by losing their link with God. This sin also brought death to their bodies. If they had eaten from the Tree of Life, everything would be different today. There would be no death. We would all be living with God. Everyone would have eternal life.

The way to the Tree of Life was cut off because Adam sinned. Then there was no way for people to have eternal life. It is a sad story, but there is good news! God did not forget us when Adam sinned. Later, He sent Jesus Christ into the world to show us the way to eternal life. So, don't be sad. Believe in Jesus and the way to the Tree of Life will open to you!

Dear God,

thank You for sending Your son, Jesus, for me!

The First Lamb Sacrifice

Abel brought the best parts from some of the firstborn
of his flock. The Lord accepted Abel and his gift,
but he did not accept Cain and his gift.

GENESIS 4:4–5 NCV

God likes good gifts, just like we do! This is a story about the first gifts given to God. One of these gifts was a lamb, which is a baby sheep. Each baby lamb makes its own high-sounding noise called bleating. This is the way the mother sheep can know her own baby lamb.

In the Bible, the first human mother, Eve, and the first human father, Adam, had a baby boy. They named him Cain. Then they had a second boy and named him Abel. Cain worked the land and raised food. Abel took care of sheep and raised lambs.

One day Cain brought some of his garden vegetables to God. This was not the offering God wanted Cain to bring. So God was not pleased with Cain and his gift. And Cain became very angry.

God said to Cain, "Why are you angry? Do what is right and bring the right kind of gift. Then I will accept your gift."

Abel brought some of the fattest parts of his best lambs as gifts for God. They were the male lambs that were born first. God was pleased with Abel and his gifts.

We don't sacrifice animals anymore. But God does want us to bring our best to Him by praying and by doing the right thing.

Dear God,

You like good gifts— just like me! I want to bring You the best that I have. Help me to always do what pleases You. Amen.

The First Prayers

That's when men and women began praying
and worshiping in the name of God.

<small>GENESIS 4:26 MSG</small>

A long time ago, God created the world. He made plants and birds and fish and animals. And then He made people. The first people were named Adam and Eve.

Adam and Eve lived in a beautiful garden called Eden. God talked with Adam and Eve in the garden. It was a perfect place. But then Adam and Eve did something wrong. They disobeyed God by eating fruit from a special tree. God had said, "Don't!"

Because they did wrong, God made Adam and Eve leave their beautiful garden. Now they had to work hard for their food. God told them that someday they would die. The wrong they did messed up everything!

Before long, Adam and Eve started a family. They had a baby boy they named Cain. Then they had another baby boy they called Abel. When the boys grew up, the wrong that Adam and Eve did caused more trouble. Cain got mad at his younger brother and killed him.

People could see that doing wrong things was a big problem. They knew that they needed help. And they knew that only God could help them.

So they started to call out to God. They asked Him for help. They prayed the first prayers. And people have been praying to God ever since.

Dear God,

I'm so glad that I can talk to You. Thank You for listening to my prayers! Amen.

"It Broke His Heart."

And he saw that all their thoughts were consistently
and totally evil. So the Lord was sorry he had
ever made them. It broke his heart.

GENESIS 6:5–6 NLT

The journey from Genesis chapter three to chapter six is not happy. But in chapter six, things get better. This chapter tells of Noah and the ark—a good story about how God solved the problem of man's wickedness. God saw how bad the people on the earth were, and He was sorry that He had made them. So He decided to destroy every living creature on the earth. "I'll wipe out people, animals, birds, and reptiles," said God.

The bright spot in this story is Noah. He was the only person who lived right and obeyed God. Everyone else, the Bible says, was terribly cruel and violent.

So God told Noah, "Get some wood and build a boat."

You may know how the rest of the story goes. The boat that Noah built was Noah's ark. Noah, his family, and animals of every kind went into the ark. Then it began to rain. It didn't stop raining for forty days! The flood destroyed everything except for what was in the ark. In the end, Noah and his family began a new world.

God judged the human race in Noah's time. He destroyed everything. But in the ark, God made a way of escape. For us today, that way is Jesus Christ.

Dear God,

thank You for sending Jesus Christ to save people in this world.

The Animals on the Ark

The clean animals, the unclean animals, the birds,
and everything that crawls on the ground came to Noah.
They went into the boat in groups of two, male and female,
just as God had commanded Noah.

GENESIS 7:8–9 NCV

There are millions and millions of different creatures living in the world today. Now imagine how big Noah's ark had to be to hold two of every animal in the world. It had to be gigantic!

Zzzz-zzz went the saws. *Bang, bang, bang* went the hammers. God told Noah to build a big boat. The people laughed at Noah when they saw such a big boat sitting on dry land. But Noah and his sons just kept on sawing and hammering.

Soon the boat was finished. God told Noah to take two of every animal into the ark. Two lions padded into the boat. Two rabbits hopped in. Two ducks waddled in. Two kangaroos jumped into the ark. Two snakes crawled in. Two hippopotamuses thumped in. Two birds flew in. Two of every kind of animal, bird, and crawling creature went into the boat.

Then Noah and his family went into the boat. And God shut the door!

It began to rain. It rained and rained and rained. The water got deeper and deeper. The big boat floated on the water. Noah believed in God's promises, and God didn't let him sink! He kept Noah's family and all the animals safe.

Dear God,

like Noah, I believe in Your promises. I know You will never let me down. So no matter what, I can be brave, just like Noah. Amen.

The Raven and the Dove

He [Noah] sent a raven out. It kept flying back
and forth until the water had dried up from the earth.
Then Noah sent a dove out.

GENESIS 8:7–8 NIrV

Ravens and doves are awesome birds. A raven has powerful wings, will eat almost anything, and can fly for a long time without resting. It makes its nest in high places. The dove also has powerful wings but stays closer to the ground and eats mostly plants. Noah used these two birds to help him find out if the floodwaters had gone down.

Noah and his family had been in the ark for many, many days. When the rain stopped, God sent a wind to blow. The water began to go down.

When the ark stopped floating, Noah opened the window and sent out a raven. The bird had mighty wings, so it flew back and forth until it found a place to rest.

Noah waited a while longer then sent out a dove. The dove came back because it could not find any place to rest. Later Noah sent out the dove again. By evening, it came back with a leaf in its bill. Noah knew the earth would soon be dry and his family and all the animals could leave the ark.

When God created birds, He knew the raven and the dove would need powerful wings for a special job. When God created you, He gave you gifts for a special job, too. Wonder what that will be.

Thank You,

God, for creating animals and people with special gifts that we can use to serve You and each other. Amen.

"Noah, His Wife, and His Sons..."

So Noah, his wife, and his sons and their wives left the boat. . . .
Then Noah built an altar to the Lord.
GENESIS 8:18, 20 NLT

Noah was six hundred years old when he went into the ark to escape the flood. All his family went inside, too. The water in the earth started gushing out everywhere. The sky opened like a window, and rain poured down for forty days and nights. The water became deeper and deeper until the boat could float.

The flood became so deep that even the highest mountains were under water! Not an animal or person was left alive anywhere on the earth. Nothing was alive except Noah and his family and the animals in the ark.

One hundred fifty days later, God made a wind blow. The rain stopped and the flooding stopped. One day the ark came to rest on a mountain. After a while, the other mountaintops could be seen. Finally, the earth was dry. Then God said, "You may now leave the ark." After Noah's family had gone out of the boat, the animals all left, too.

What a terrible time that must have been! And when it was all over, what was the first thing Noah did? He worshipped God. Noah is your example. He teaches you that no matter what happens, remember to worship God.

Dear God,

help me to remember to worship You— no matter what happens in my life.

"I Am Giving You a Sign."

And God said, "I am giving you a sign. . . . I have placed my
rainbow in the clouds. . . . Never again
will there be a flood that will destroy all life."

GENESIS 9:12–13, 15 NLT

Do you like to see a rainbow in the sky? They are so beautiful! Do you know what makes a rainbow? Sun shining through falling rain. But in Noah's time, there had never been a rainbow before. The rains that brought the flood were the first rains ever. When Noah saw the rains ending, the sun came out. Then Noah and his family saw the very first rainbow ever, and they knew they had survived the Great Flood.

Imagine what Noah's family felt the next time rain clouds came. They must have been afraid of the rain. After all, the first time it rained, the flood destroyed the whole earth! But God didn't want them to be afraid. God promised Noah and his family that He would never again destroy the earth with a flood. Rainbows are a reminder that this promise is true. God has kept this promise to Noah. Since the time of Noah, floods have never destroyed the whole earth. Remember this whenever you see a rainbow.

The Bible tells many of God's promises. All these are as real and beautiful as a rainbow. And all of them are true!

Dear God,

thank You for
always keeping
Your word!

Moving Day

"I will make you a great nation, and I will bless you.
I will make you famous. And you will be a blessing to others."

GENESIS 12:2 ICB

Have you ever moved to a new place? In the Bible book of Genesis, God told Abraham to move away from all his friends. But He didn't tell Abraham where to go. He just said He would show him. Because God knew it would be hard for Abraham to leave his home, He gave him a special blessing to cheer him up. God said, "I will make you a great nation, and I will bless you. I will make you famous. And you will be a blessing to others."

Abraham didn't have to make that big move to a new place all alone. God went with him to help him. He even made Abraham a blessing to the new people he met. Abraham knew that God's plan for his life was good. He trusted God to do what was best for him. And God did!

Wherever you go, God goes with you. He always has a good plan for your life. He'll help you make new friends and be a special blessing to them. God is your forever friend no matter where you go.

God, being in a new place can be scary. Help me to trust You and the good plan You have for me. Thanks for being my forever friend.

An Animal Offering to God

The Lord said to Abram, "Bring me a three-year-old cow,
a three-year-old goat, a three-year-old male sheep,
a dove and a young pigeon."

GENESIS 15:9 NCV

In the Old Testament, God asked people to sacrifice animals. Sometimes those sacrifices were made to worship God. Sometimes they stood for a promise from God to a man.

God made a promise to Abram one day. He came to Abram in a vision and told him that he would be blessed. Then God took Abram outside and said, "Look up at the sky. Count the stars, if you can. You will have that many children."

Abram believed God. God asked Abram to bring some animals to Him—a three-year-old cow, a three-year-old goat, a three-year-old male sheep, a dove, and a young pigeon—for a sacrifice.

Abram brought the animals to God and cut them into two pieces. As the sun was going down in the sky, Abram fell into a deep sleep. Soon it was dark all around. A burning torch and a firepot filled with smoke appeared. They passed between the pieces of the animals.

God made a promise to Abram on that day. He would bless Abram's children and their children and all the children who came later.

God promises to bless you and all His other children today—but an animal sacrifice is not needed.

God,

I'm glad I am Your child. Thank You for blessing me. Amen.

A Ram Is Provided

Abraham looked up and there in a thicket he saw a ram caught by its horns. He went over and took the ram and sacrificed it as a burnt offering instead of his son.

GENESIS 22:13 NIV

A male sheep is called a *ram*. Rams have horns to fight off wild animals and other male sheep. In the Bible, rams were used as a sacrifice offering. One day God asked Abraham to make a sacrifice offering.

God spoke to Abraham. "Take your son, Isaac, to a place I will show you. Give your son as an offering to Me."

Abraham loved God, but giving up his only son, Isaac, was a very hard thing to do. Abraham loved Isaac but he did not argue with God. He took Isaac with him to the mountain God showed him.

On the climb up the mountain, Isaac asked, "Father, we have the wood and fire, but where is the offering?"

Abraham answered, "God will give us one."

Isaac helped Abraham build an altar. Then Abraham laid his son on the altar as an offering, just as God had asked. Suddenly God's angel spoke. "Abraham! Do not hurt your son." Abraham looked up and saw a ram. Its horns had gotten caught in a bush. Instead of sacrificing his son, Abraham sacrificed the ram God had provided.

God provided the ram for Isaac. Later God provided Jesus for the whole world. When our hearts obey and trust in God, He always delivers—no matter what!

Dear God,

sometimes I'm asked to do something hard—even something I don't want to do. Give me courage to obey You because You always know what is best. Amen.

Camels at Rebekah's Well

After he finished drinking, Rebekah said,
"I will also pour some water for your camels."
GENESIS 24:19 NCV

A camel is a good animal for traveling through the hot, dry desert. The camel can go without water for a long time. It can carry a heavy load on its hump just like it did for Abraham's servant.

Abraham called his servant to him. "Go into a far country to find a wife for my son, Isaac," he said. "God will go ahead of you and show you what to do."

So the servant loaded camels with gifts and traveled to a far country. He stopped near a well outside town and made the thirsty camels kneel down. Then he waited for the women to come to the well for water.

"God, show me the young woman to whom I will speak," prayed the servant. "If she gives me a drink and waters my camels, I will know that is the one You have chosen for Isaac."

Before long, Rebekah came to the well for water. She gave the servant a drink and then said, "I will also give your camels a drink."

The servant knew Rebekah was the wife God had picked for Isaac.

God uses many things of this world to guide us. Here He used camels and a praying servant. Lift your prayers to God, then look for His guidance.

Dear God,

I know that You will always answer my prayers. Thank You for showing me what to do when I ask. Help me to follow Your answer. Amen.

Praying for Your Family

Isaac's wife could not have children,
so Isaac prayed to the Lord for her.
The Lord heard Isaac's prayer.
GENESIS 25:21 NCV

God wants us to pray for each of our family members—Mom, Dad, sisters and brothers, grandparents, aunts and uncles, and cousins. Isaac asked God to give his wife, Rebekah, something she wanted—children. And God heard his prayer.

Isaac knew that Rebekah wanted a child. No one knew why, but she had not had any babies. Abraham, Isaac's father, loved and worshipped God. He taught Isaac to pray to God about everything. So he prayed. "God, Rebekah is a good wife. I love her very much. Would You please give her what she wants most—a baby of her own?"

God answered Isaac's prayer in a special way. Soon Rebekah learned that she was going to have a baby. And not just one but two! She was going to have twins. She could tell because she could feel them tumbling around inside her.

Soon the day came when Rebekah had the babies. First came one boy. Isaac and Rebekah named him Esau. Then came another boy. They named him Jacob. The boys grew. Isaac and Rebekah were happy with their new family. Isaac thanked God for answering his prayer.

Dear heavenly Father,

thank You for my family— Mom, Dad, sisters, and brothers. Help me remember to pray for each one of them every day. Amen.

Blessed by Accident

"May God give you plenty of rain and good soil.
Then you will have plenty of grain and wine."

GENESIS 27:28 ICB

Isaac had twin sons, Jacob and Esau. Even though they were twins, Esau was born a few minutes before Jacob, so he was the oldest, and the oldest son was supposed to get the father's blessing. But their mother, Rebekah, wanted their father to bless Jacob instead of Esau, so she came up with a plan.

Isaac was old and almost blind. Rebekah told Jacob to cook Isaac's favorite food and dress up like Esau to trick Isaac. Then Isaac would think Jacob was Esau and would bless him.

Their plan worked. Isaac smelled Esau's clothes on Jacob and thought it was his oldest son. Isaac knew God was the only One who could always provide everything we need, so he blessed Jacob, saying, "May God give you plenty of rain and good soil. Then you will have plenty of grain and wine."

It's not right to trick people as Jacob did. Before God could bless him, Jacob had to move far from home. He lived in fear of Esau's anger. But later Jacob humbled himself before God. He tried to make things right with Esau. Then God could give Jacob his father's blessing.

Just as God gave rain, good soil, and food to Jacob, God will provide for your needs, too. What do you need today?

God,
sometimes I do things I shouldn't. Thanks for promising that You'll take care of me even when I make mistakes. I love You.

"Deliver Me from Destruction"

O Lord, please deliver me from destruction
at the hand of my brother Esau, for I am frightened—
terribly afraid that he is coming to kill me.

GENESIS 32:11 TLB

When we are afraid someone will hurt us, we can pray. Jacob asked God to keep him safe when he was afraid his brother, Esau, would hurt him.

One day Jacob stole something important from his brother. He knew that Esau wanted to hurt him for that—so Jacob ran away.

Many years later, God told Jacob to go back home. Jacob and his family packed their things for the long trip. Jacob sent some helpers to tell Esau that he wanted to come home for a visit.

The helpers came back and said, "We saw Esau. He is coming to meet you with four hundred men!"

Jacob was afraid. Four hundred men sounded like an army! So Jacob prayed for God to keep him and his family safe.

Jacob decided to send Esau some presents. After all, he was the one who had stolen from Esau.

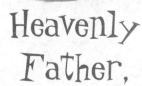

Step, step, step! Jacob and his family walked. Finally, they saw Esau and his four hundred men coming!

As Jacob walked toward Esau, he bowed over and over to show he was sorry for the wrong things he had done. Esau ran toward Jacob. Jacob wondered if Esau was going to hurt him. But Esau grabbed Jacob and gave him a hug.

Heavenly Father,

thank You for keeping me safe when someone wants to hurt me. Help me remember that You will always take care of me. Amen.

Rubbed-Off Blessing

Then the Lord blessed the people in
Potiphar's house because of Joseph.

GENESIS 39:5 ICB

Have you ever had something rub off on you? Maybe when you ate a chocolate bar your face or fingers ended up all chocolaty. Or maybe the picture you drew with a marker was still wet when you put your hand on it. Then you saw that you had the marker color on your hand!

A man named Potiphar put Joseph in charge of everything he owned. Joseph loved God and lived to serve Him. He worked hard and did his best at taking care of Potiphar's things. This made God happy, so He caused Joseph to do well at everything he did.

But then a funny thing happened. God's blessing on Joseph started rubbing off on Potiphar and his whole family. Everything Potiphar did went well because of the good work Joseph did. Joseph's blessing became Potiphar's blessing, too!

Has one of your friends ever had good things happen because of you? If you love God, you will try to please Him by the way you live. Then His blessing may rub off of you and onto your friends! Wouldn't that be a nice gift to give a friend?

I love You, God, and want Your blessing. Please bless my friends because of my faith in You, just as You did with Joseph and Potiphar.

Brothers' Blessings

"Judah, your brothers will praise you. You will grab your enemies by the neck. Your brothers will bow down to you."

GENESIS 49:8 ICB

Jacob had twelve sons. That's a big family! When he was old and about to die, Jacob asked all his sons to gather around him. He wanted to tell them what would happen to them in the future. For some of his sons, it was bad news. For others, like Judah, it was good.

"Judah." Jacob's voice was probably low as he lifted a weak hand and motioned for his son to come closer. "Your brothers will praise you. You will grab your enemies by the neck. Your brothers will bow down to you." He also said that Judah was brave like a lion and would be a great leader. Entire nations would obey him. Judah and his sons would always be king until the real King, Jesus, came to earth.

How would you feel if your brothers or sisters praised you, saying wonderful things about you, as Jacob said Judah's brothers would? Maybe they already do! It's good to get along with brothers and sisters, but it's not always easy. And it's even harder to get along with your enemies, people you don't like. Ask God to help you behave in a way that earns their praise!

Lord, sometimes I fight with my brothers and sisters. Help me to get along with them when we play. And show me how to be nice to my enemies.

"It's Not Fair!"

"Dan will do what is fair for his people."
Genesis 49:16 NIrV

In our Bibles, we learn Dan was one of twelve boys. When his father, Jacob, grew old and was ready to die, he gave blessings to his sons. He called them to his bedside one by one so they could receive their blessings. He started with Reuben, the oldest, and went clear down to the youngest, Benjamin. Dan was the seventh brother. I bet he could hardly wait his turn! What would his father say about his future?

"Dan," Jacob began, "you will do what is fair for your people." Dan may have smiled. His father trusted him! Jacob knew his son was honest and treated people fairly. That must have made Dan feel proud.

Are you fair to people? Do you take turns? Are you a good sport, or do you cry, "It's not fair!" when you don't win? Do you do what you say you'll do? If you can answer yes to all these questions, good for you! But if you had to say no to some, don't worry. God will help you become the boy or girl He wants you to be if you ask for His help.

God,

I want to be someone people trust, but I can't do it by myself. Will You please help me to be honest and fair? Thanks!

Growing a Seed

"Asher's land will grow much good food.
He will grow food fit for a king."

Genesis 49:20 ICB

Asher, whose name meant "happy," was Jacob's ninth son. He waited to hear what his dying father's blessing for him would be. Would it be wealth? Ruling nations? Good health? Finally, it was his turn.

"Asher, my son. Your land will grow lots of good food. It will be food good enough to feed kings!"

Back in Bible times, most people were farmers. It was important for them to have good land to grow food to feed their families. But to have land good enough to grow delicious food for important kings? Well, that was a very special blessing that made Asher as happy as his name! He probably started learning to farm by planting a few seeds and watching them grow. His parents might have had to remind him to water his seeds and take care of them. He may have found that he really liked cooking and eating the food he grew.

You can be like Asher and grow food, too. Try planting a bean in a cup with some dirt. Set it in a sunny place by a window and water it a little when the soil gets dry. Maybe you'll enjoy growing things like Asher did.

Lord,
help my seeds to grow.
But more important than
that, help me to grow into
a person who lives for You.
Teach me to be my best
for You.

The Great Outdoors

Naphtali is a deer running free that gives birth to lovely fawns.

GENESIS 49:21 MSG

Are you ever compared to an animal? Maybe your parents have said you're a monkey because you like to climb on things. Or a honey bunny because you give good hugs. Or maybe on a grouchy morning they even called you a growly bear!

Naphtali's dad, Jacob, blessed him by saying he was a deer running free that gives birth to lovely fawns. He had watched his son grow from a boy to a man. He knew he loved to be outdoors and run in the fresh air. He loved the freedom the big outdoors offered.

Just as Naphtali wasn't *really* a deer, he didn't *really* give birth to lovely fawns either. Jacob probably meant that his son was creative and made many beautiful things. Or maybe he was someone who tenderly cared for others as a mother would care for her children. Either way, it's clear that Jacob loved his son and was proud of him.

Do you like to play outside? Do you run fast and enjoy the wind blowing in your hair? Do you make beautiful things or lovingly care for others? Then you're like Naphtali! But however God made you, He loves you very much!

Thank You,

God, for the awesome world You made for us to enjoy. Help me to take good care of it and the people around me.

Strong for Him

Thank You, God, for giving me strength.

"He gets his power from
the Mighty God of Jacob."

GENESIS 49:24 ICB

Joseph was the little brother to ten older brothers. But his father, Jacob, liked Joseph the most. It wasn't right, but the Bible says that's the way it was. Because Jacob loved Joseph best, he gave him a special blessing.

He said Joseph was strong even when people weren't nice to him. But most important, Jacob told Joseph, "Your power comes from the Mighty God of Jacob. And your strength comes from the Shepherd, the Rock of Israel" (Genesis 49:25 ICB).

We know God's the only One who can give us real strength and power and so did Joseph. We're like an electrical cord that is plugged into our power outlet—God.

Joseph may have felt that he wasn't very strong or brave compared to his big brothers. Sometimes we feel we can't do anything right. Or that we aren't big enough to do important things. But when we pray and read the Bible, we plug into the greatest power source—God. And, like Joseph, we can do amazing things.

Believe in God. He'll make you strong and powerful. You won't feel so small anymore—you'll feel like a giant!

Help me

to trust You, God.
There are lots of things
I can't do yet, but I
know You'll help me
to be strong for You.

Moses Takes Care of the Sheep

Moses was shepherding the flock of Jethro, his father-in-law, the priest of Midian. He led the flock to the west end of the wilderness and came to the mountain of God, Horeb.

EXODUS 3:1 MSG

Sheep are cute but not very smart. They are helpless and need lots of protection. A group of sheep is called a *flock,* and the person who takes care of them is called a *shepherd.* Sheep were important to families in Bible times because they provided milk and meat, as well as wool to make tents and clothing.

Moses was the shepherd of his father-in-law's sheep. He led them to good water and delicious grass. Moses carried a big stick called a *staff* or *crook* to help guide and protect his flock.

One day while the shepherd Moses was out in the wilderness, he saw a burning bush. Moses was curious, so he came closer.

God spoke from the bush. "Moses! Moses!"

"Here I am," Moses said.

"Don't come any closer," God said. "Take off your sandals. The place you are standing is holy ground. I am your God."

When Moses heard this, he turned his face away. He was afraid to look at God.

"Go back to Egypt and help the people there," said God. "Bring them out of the land and to a land that I will give them."

Before Moses did what God asked, he made sure that his flock had a new shepherd. We have a good shepherd, too. His name is Jesus.

Dear God,

thank You for Jesus, my Good Shepherd. Help me to follow Him always. Amen.

The Stick Becomes a Snake

Aaron threw his staff down in front of Pharaoh
and his officials. It turned into a snake.

EXODUS 7:10 NIrV

Snakes can be very tricky. Sometimes they blend in with the things around them, making them hard to see. This makes it easy for them to catch mice, birds, and frogs. Some snakes look like a stick. This story is about Aaron's stick (or shepherd's staff) that turned into a snake.

Moses was taking care of the sheep when God spoke to him. "Moses, go back to Egypt. The pharaoh is causing much trouble to My people. Ask Pharaoh to let the people go free."

God sent Moses and his brother, Aaron, to help the people get away from the bad pharaoh. When Pharaoh would not let the people go free, God told Moses and Aaron what to do to show God's power. "Throw your staff down in front of Pharaoh. It will become a snake."

So they went back to Pharaoh. Aaron threw his stick down. It turned into a snake, just as God said it would.

Then Pharaoh called his magicians, and they turned their sticks into snakes, too. But Aaron's snake swallowed all the other snakes!

Snakes usually frighten people, but Pharaoh was not scared. He still would not let God's people leave Egypt.

Dear God,

You are wiser and more powerful than any magician. Help me to be smart, like You, not stubborn, like Pharaoh. Amen.

Frogs Everywhere

So Aaron held his hand over all the waters of Egypt, and the
frogs came up out of the water and covered the land of Egypt.

EXODUS 8:6 NCV

Did you know that a frog can jump twenty times its own length? That's pretty far! When Aaron stretched his stick over the water, frogs began to jump everywhere.

God sent Moses and his brother, Aaron, to ask Pharaoh to let the people of Israel go free. When Pharaoh would not let them go, God told Moses what to do.

"Tell Aaron to hold his stick over the rivers and ponds," said God. "The frogs will come onto the land."

Aaron did as Moses told him. Frogs came out of the rivers and ponds. There were big frogs and little frogs. The frogs covered the land. There were frogs in the houses. There were frogs in the beds and on the chairs. People sat on the frogs. They walked on the frogs. Frogs jumped on the tables. Frogs plopped in the food. The frogs jumped on Pharaoh and his people. But the frogs did not bother God's people.

The pharaoh called for Moses. "Take away the frogs," the king said. "I will let the people go." But Pharaoh did not keep his word.

God is not like Pharaoh. He *always* keeps His word. Now that's something to jump up and down about!

Thank You, God, for frogs. And thank You for always keeping Your word. It makes me jump for joy! Amen.

Dust Becomes Lice

So the Lord said to Moses, "Say to Aaron, 'Stretch out your rod, and strike the dust of the land, so that it may become lice throughout all the land of Egypt.'"

EXODUS 8:16 NKJV

Lice are ugly insects. They have hook-shaped claws and strong legs that hang on to hair. Lice crawl down the hair and make the skin itch. There must have been many itchy people and animals when God sent the lice to the people of Egypt!

For many years, God's people had been slaves to Pharaoh. God sent Moses and Aaron to Pharaoh many times but the Egyptian king would not let the people go free.

Once more Moses and Aaron asked Pharaoh to let the people go. And once again, Pharaoh said, "No!"

"Moses, tell Aaron to stretch out his staff," God said. "Tell him to strike the dust. It will turn to lice."

So Aaron did what Moses told him to do. When Aaron hit the dust with his stick, little bugs were everywhere. The lice hopped on the animals. They hopped on Pharaoh and his people.

Scratch, scratch, scratch went the people! *Scratch, scratch, scratch* went Pharaoh! *Scratch, scratch, scratch* went the animals! The lice made all the people and animals itch. But Pharaoh still would not let God's people go.

God can use any insect—even the ugly, tiny lice—to get people to obey Him.

God,

You are Master of everything—including me! Help me to listen and then do what You say. Amen.

A Swarm of Flies

"If you don't let them go, I will send swarms of flies into your houses. The flies will be on you, your officers, and your people. The houses of Egypt will be full of flies, and they will be all over the ground, too."

Exodus 8:21 NCV

Flies are very icky insects. They have sticky pads on their feet, which helps them walk on the walls and ceiling. They also carry harmful germs. So the flies that God sent to the pharaoh and his people caused great problems.

God's people were slaves to Pharaoh. God wanted His people to go free so they could worship Him. He sent Moses and Aaron to talk to Pharaoh.

"Let God's people go with me so they can worship Him," said Moses to Pharaoh. "If you don't let the people go, God will send flies to cover the land."

But Pharaoh said, "No!"

So God sent a swarm of flies, just like He said He would do. The flies were everywhere. The ground was covered with flies. They were in Pharaoh's palace. In the houses, the flies walked on the walls and ceilings. They got into the food. People were swatting the flies, but the icky insects would not go away.

Even when the flies were everywhere and bringing disease to the people, Pharaoh still said, "No, I will not let the people go."

God can use any way and anything—even the pesky fly—to get someone's attention.

Dear God,

You have my attention. Show me how I can be useful to You.

Amen.

The Livestock Die

"If you refuse to let them go. . .the Lord will bring a terrible plague on your livestock in the field—on your horses, donkeys and camels and on your cattle, sheep and goats."

EXODUS 9:2–3 NIV

The word *livestock* means the animals that live on the farm. They include cattle, horses, donkeys, goats, and sheep—even camels! Livestock was and still is important. Cattle, goats, and sheep give people meat, milk, and material for clothing. And horses, donkeys, and camels are used to carry things and people.

Moses and his brother, Aaron, had been to see Pharaoh several times. They had asked him to let God's people go free. But each time, Pharaoh would not let the people go with Moses. God had turned the river into blood. He had brought frogs to cover the land. He had caused the dust to change into lice. He had brought a large number of flies to destroy the land. But Pharaoh would not let the people go.

"If you do not let the people go this time," Moses told Pharaoh, "all the livestock—horses, donkeys, camels, cattle, sheep, and goats—will die."

Pharaoh said, "No!"

The next day, all the livestock of Pharaoh and his people died. Now the people would not have the good things that the livestock would have provided. But once again, Pharaoh would not let the people go.

God created each kind of livestock for a special job. Without each one of them, people would not have their daily needs met.

Thank You, God, for farm animals and all the things they provide. And thank You for taking care of me every day. Amen.

The Locusts Arrive

The Lord told Moses, "Raise your hand over the land of Egypt, and the locusts will come. They will spread all over the land of Egypt and will eat all the plants the hail did not destroy."

EXODUS 10:12 NCV

A desert locust is a powerful jumper. Because of its strong legs, it can jump forty times the length of its body! Sometimes locusts come in big groups called *swarms.* Some swarms have as many as a billion locusts! That's a lot of locusts! They have sharp teeth and can eat a lot, just as they did in the land of Egypt.

Moses and his brother, Aaron, had been to Pharaoh many times. They had asked him to let God's people go free. Each time, Pharaoh said, "No!"

Once again God told Moses to talk to Pharaoh, and once again he said, "No, they cannot go free!"

God told Moses, "Raise your hand over Egypt. Locusts will cover the land and eat everything that is growing in the fields."

So Moses did what God told him to do. Immediately, locusts covered the land.

Munch, munch, munch! They ate up everything that was growing in the fields. *Munch, munch!* They ate the fruit on the trees. Nothing green was left on the trees or plants.

Pharaoh called for Moses. "Take away the locusts," Pharaoh said. "I will let the people go." But Pharaoh did not keep his word.

Dear God,

I don't want to be like Pharaoh. Please help me to keep my word to You and others. Amen.

"The Lord Guided Them."

The Lord guided them by a pillar of cloud during
the day and a pillar of fire at night.
EXODUS 13:21 NLT

When the children of Israel escaped Egypt, they knew exactly which way to go. The Lord guided them day and night. During the day, they followed a pillar of cloud. At night, it became a pillar of fire. This pillar may have looked like a huge pine tree that was made out of cloud and fire.

Even though they knew God was leading them, the Israelites were often afraid and tired of their journey. Once they came to a place called Rephidim. There was no water there, so they complained to Moses, "Give us water to drink!" They were sorry they'd ever left Egypt and thought that they would die.

Moses didn't know what to do. "What should I do with these people?" he cried to God. "They are about to stone me!"

"Take your shepherd's staff and walk ahead of the people," the Lord answered. "I'll meet you by the rock at Mount Sinai. Strike the rock, and water will come pouring out." Sure enough, water gushed out of the rock.

Today, Jesus Christ is like that rock. He provides the water that we need to never be thirsty again. He said, "But the water I give them takes away thirst altogether. It becomes a perpetual spring within them, giving them eternal life."

Dear God,
thank You for
Your son, Jesus,
who gives us
eternal life.

Pharaoh's Horses and Chariots

The Egyptians chased them. All of Pharaoh's horses and chariots and horsemen followed them into the sea.

Exodus 14:23 NIrV

Horses are used for many things—riding for fun, police work, farm work, and more. In Bible times, horses were used to pull chariots.

God struck Egypt with ten plagues. Then Pharaoh finally said, "Yes!" when Moses asked him to let God's people go. Moses led God's people out of Egypt, where Pharaoh had kept them as slaves. They traveled day and night. God guided them by a pillar of cloud during the day and a pillar of fire at night.

After God's people left, Pharaoh changed his mind. He wanted them back. He told his men to go after God's people with horses and chariots.

When God's people stopped by the sea, they saw Pharaoh's men coming behind them. They were scared. They had nowhere to run. The water was in front of them, and Pharaoh's men were behind them.

"Don't be afraid," said Moses. "God will take care of you." Moses raised his hands over the water.

Something amazing happened! God caused the wind to push the water back so the people could walk on dry ground. When all the people had crossed, the water flowed back together. Pharaoh's men, horses, and chariots tried to escape but were swallowed by the sea.

Pharaoh wanted to harm God's people, but our God kept them safe with His awesome power.

Dear God,

You are more powerful than anyone on earth. Thank You for watching over me all day and night, awake and asleep! Amen.

A Special Piece of Wood

Moses cried out to the Lord, and the Lord
showed him a piece of wood.

EXODUS 15:25 NIV

When we need help with a problem, we can pray. Even when Moses and God's people were in the desert without water, God answered Moses' cry for help.

Have you ever been hot and thirsty? Long ago, God's people were hot and thirsty. They could not find a drop of cool water to drink.

God's people were on a long trip. They walked through the hot desert. There were very few trees for shade. There was no water to drink, but there was a lot of hot sand. God's people walked across the hot, hot sand. Step, step, step!

For three days, God's people had no water. "We are thirsty!" they grumbled to Moses, their leader.

Then someone shouted, "Water!"

The people saw the clear, cool water. They ran to it and took big drinks.

"Yuck! This water tastes bad," they complained. "We can't drink this water."

Moses heard the grumbling people. He asked God what to do. God told Moses to throw a special piece of wood into the water. *Splash!*

The special piece of wood made the water taste good. Everyone began to drink, slowly at first. They drank faster as they realized how good it tasted.

Moses was happy. God had showed him what to do to help the thirsty people.

Dear God,

thank You for giving me cool water to drink. Help me to pray when I have a problem. I know You will always answer my prayer.

Amen.

God Sent Quail

That evening quail came and covered the camp. In the morning
the ground around the camp was covered with dew.

EXODUS 16:13 NIrV

Quail are short, stocky birds. Because their wings are short, they must beat them rapidly to fly. They spend much of their life on the ground, running and zigzagging through the grass. This made it easier for God's hungry people to gather the quail to eat when God provided this bird.

God's people were moving to a new home. They had brought food with them, but now the food was almost gone. There were no stores to buy more food.

The people began to grumble to Moses, their leader. "We are hungry," they said. "If we had stayed in Egypt, we would have plenty to eat. We will die without food. What shall we do?"

Moses talked to God. Then he told the people what God had said. "In the evening, you will see the glory of God. God isn't happy with all your grumbling, but He will take care of you."

That night God sent many quail to the people's camp. Now the people had plenty of meat to eat. They were happy because God took care of them. The people thanked God for His gift of food—the quail.

Dear God,

help me not to be grumpy and complain about things. Remind me that You will always give me whatever I need. Thank You. Amen.

Water from a Rock

Moses cried out to the Lord,
"What am I to do with these people?"
EXODUS 17:4 NIV

When someone wants to argue with us, we can pray and ask God what He wants us to do. God's people argued with Moses, and he talked to God about all their arguing and complaining.

God had chosen Moses to lead the people to a new land. He had guarded them from the great armies that wanted to destroy them. God had given them food when they were hungry. Now they were in the desert.

"Give us water to drink," the people demanded.

"Why are you always arguing with me?" asked Moses. "Don't you know God will take care of us?"

But the people kept shouting.

Moses talked to God. "What do You want me to do?" he prayed.

God answered Moses and said, "Walk ahead of the people. Take some of the older leaders with you. Take the staff with you. When you come to a big rock, strike the rock with your staff. Water will come out of the rock."

So Moses did what God told him to do. When the people came to the rock, there was fresh water for them to drink. Moses was thankful that God heard his prayer and gave the people what they needed.

Dear God,

tell me what to do when people around me argue and grumble. Help me tell them that You love them and can make them happy. Amen.

"Help Me to Know You, Lord"

"If you are pleased with me, teach me more about yourself.
Then I can know you. And I can continue to please you."
Exodus 33:13 NIrV

When you want to know about your friend, you spend time with that friend. By spending time in prayer, you can learn more about God. Moses wanted to know more about God so he spent more time praying to Him. That's when God told Moses about the important things He wanted Moses to do.

Moses led God's people away from the king of Egypt, who was unkind to them. Moses asked God to give the people fresh water to drink when they were thirsty. He asked God for food to eat when they were hungry. God gave Moses the Ten Commandments to help the people know how they could please God.

After Moses heard about all the things God wanted him to do, he spent even more time talking to God. He wanted to know more so that he could please God in everything he did.

Whenever Moses had a problem, he talked to God about it. God always helped him know what to do. Moses became a very great leader. All the people respected him and listened to him. Even the king of Egypt listened. He didn't want to, but he finally let God's people follow Moses.

God,
just like Moses,
I want to know You.
Help me spend more
time with You in prayer.
Thank You for always
being near me. Amen.

Clean and Unclean Creatures

The Lord said to Moses and Aaron, "Tell the Israelites this:
'These are the land animals you may eat.'"

LEVITICUS 11:1–2 NCV

The Old Testament says it's okay if you eat grasshoppers! Gross!

Long ago, God gave Moses special instructions and laws which told God's people what creatures they could eat. The clean creatures could be eaten; the unclean creatures could not be eaten.

Land animals that chew the cud and have hooves that are separated completely in two are clean and can be eaten. Some of those kinds of animals are the oxen, sheep, goats, and deer.

Many creatures live in the water. Those that have fins and scales can be eaten. Most of the birds of the air are unclean and not to be eaten.

The insects that fly and also walk on all four legs are not clean, unless they have joints in their legs and can hop. The insects that are clean to eat are the locusts, grasshoppers, katydids, and crickets. Yuck!

The laws in the Old Testament even told the people not to touch the unclean creatures. If an unclean creature falls on something, that item is not clean. That item must be put into water until evening, and then it will be clean.

The Israelites were God's people, and He wanted them to be pure and spotless when they worshipped Him. God made many laws that helped the people live happy, healthy lives.

Dear God,

thank You for the food that I eat. Help me to eat things that are good for me, but maybe not grasshoppers! Amen.

The Two Goats

"Next Aaron will take the two goats and bring them before the Lord at the entrance to the Meeting Tent."

LEVITICUS 16:7 NCV

Goats are strong animals that can live almost anywhere. In Bible times, goats lived in the desert and were very important to a family. A goat provided milk and meat. The goat's hair made tents. The goat's hide made water bags.

In the Bible, male goats were used as sacrifices. Once a year, two male goats were brought to the Meeting Tent. God told the priest which goat would be offered to Him and which goat would be sent away. These two goats were used as offerings for the people's sins (the wrong things people did).

One goat was killed and burned on the altar. The priest would take some of the goat's blood and enter a special place called the Holy of Holies. The Holy of Holies was inside the Meeting Tent. This was a place God had set aside for the sacrifice. The priest asked God to receive the blood and offering to forgive the sins of the people.

Then the priest would send the live goat into the wilderness. This goat was called a *scapegoat*. The goat was left to wander about. This was to show the people that their sins were taken away.

Long before Jesus, God showed humans the meaning of forgiveness through the two goats.

Dear God,

thank You for sending Jesus to die on the cross for my sins. Thank You for forgiving me when I do something wrong. You're wonderful! Amen.

The Snake on a Pole

The Lord said to Moses, "Make a bronze snake, and put it on a pole. When anyone who is bitten looks at it, that person will live."

NUMBERS 21:8 NCV

There are many different kinds of poisonous snakes. Some live along the riverbanks, in the woods, in the deserts, or in the mountains. One day God sent poisonous snakes to the desert when His people were complaining.

Moses had led God's special people away from the bad pharaoh in Egypt where they had been slaves. Now they were angry with God and complaining to Moses.

"Why have you brought us to the desert to die?" they asked. "We have no bread or water. We hate the food God has given us."

So God sent poisonous snakes. They bit the people. Many of the people died.

The people came to Moses and said, "We did wrong when we grumbled to you and to God. We are sorry. Ask God to take away the snakes."

God told Moses to make a bronze snake and put it on a pole. "Anyone who is bitten by a snake can look on the bronze snake and live."

So Moses made a bronze snake and put it on a pole. When a snake bit someone, that person looked at the bronze snake and lived.

Today we don't need to look at a bronze snake. If we ever feel the bite of sin, all we have to do is look to Jesus. He'll save us!

Dear God,
help me not to grumble when I don't get what I want. And thank You for Jesus. He's the best Savior ever. Amen.

The Donkey Talks

The Lord made the donkey talk, and she said to Balaam,
"What have I done to make you hit me three times?"

NUMBERS 22:28 NCV

Donkeys love to roll over on the ground. One day a man named Balaam had a donkey. She didn't roll over, but she did do some unusual things.

One day a king sent a message to Balaam. He would make Balaam rich if he would cause some bad things to happen to God's people.

Balaam saddled his donkey and traveled to see the bad king. God was angry with Balaam. So He sent an angel to block Balaam's way. The donkey left the road when she saw the angel. Balaam hit the donkey and got back on the road.

When the donkey saw the angel standing between two walls, she moved toward one wall. Balaam's foot was crushed. He hit the donkey again.

The third time the donkey saw the angel, she lay down. Balaam hit the donkey again.

God opened the donkey's mouth. "What have I done to make you hit me three times?" she said.

When Balaam started explaining why, God let him see the angel. The angel told Balaam if the donkey had not turned away every time she saw the angel, the angel would have killed Balaam but saved the donkey!

Animals have their own way of communicating with each other and us. But if God needed an animal to actually talk, it would. God can do all things.

Dear God,

You are truly the Master of me and all animals. Help me to be gentle with every living thing. Amen.

Superhero

"God isn't a mere man. He can't lie.
He isn't a human being.
He doesn't change his mind."

Numbers 23:19 NIrV

Who's your favorite superhero? What special powers does he or she have? There's a superhero that's stronger, more powerful, and more awesome than any other. God is the best superhero of all. Our Bible verse in Numbers 23:19 says God isn't a human like us. Here's the best part—He can't lie. And He doesn't change His mind.

Humans may seem strong sometimes. But all humans can get sick or hurt and even die. And no matter how good a human is, everyone sins and lies at some time. But not God. He never gets sick or hurt. And He'll never die, because He's immortal. That means He *can't* die. God never sins or lies or does anything wrong. We can trust Him completely. When He says something, it will happen. He doesn't change His mind. God says in John 3:16 that He loved the world so much that He gave us His one and only Son. That means He always loves us, no matter what we do or how good or bad we are. He won't change His mind.

Now that's a superhero who's worth worshipping!

Thanks for being a superhero that I can always trust, God. I'm glad You don't lie or change Your mind. I love You.

Promise Keeper

So know that the Lord your God is God. He is the faithful God.
He will keep his agreement of love for a thousand lifetimes.
He does this for people who love him and obey his commands.

DEUTERONOMY 7:9 ICB

Has someone ever broken a promise to you? I hope not, but if they did, how did it make you feel?

There is Someone you can always count on to keep His promises to you. God has never, ever broken a promise to anyone. And He never will. Our Bible verse in Deuteronomy says that He is the faithful God. That means you can depend on what He says. If He says it, then it will happen. He'll keep His promise of love for "a thousand lifetimes"! Who does He do that for? Everyone who loves Him and obeys His commands.

I know you love God. And I bet you try to obey what the Bible teaches, too. Sometimes you may not do it exactly right, but God understands that everyone makes mistakes. He loves you anyway and still keeps His promises to you. Keep loving God and trying to do what He says in His Word, and He will be proud of you.

God is the greatest promise keeper in the world. You can count on Him to be there for you every time.

Lord,

I'm glad I can be sure You'll keep Your promises. Help me to love You more and more and follow Your commands.

Blessings or Curses

Today I'm letting you
choose a blessing or a curse.

DEUTERONOMY 11:26 ICB

Moses had a big job to do. God asked him to lead His chosen people, called Israelites, out of Egypt, where they had been slaves and were treated mean. Three million people! Moses didn't think he could do it. But God said, "I'll help you."

So Moses said yes.

As the people wandered in the desert, God gave Moses the Ten Commandments. These were rules to teach them how God wanted them to live. Moses told the Israelites God's rules. Then he said, "Today I'm letting you choose a blessing or a curse. You will be blessed if you obey God's rules. But you will be cursed if you don't obey them." A blessing means good things will happen to you. A curse means bad things will happen.

God gives us the same choice today. We can choose to obey Him and do our best to live the way He wants us to, or we can choose to do things our own way. Depending on the choice we make, we will be blessed by God or cursed by Him. God loves to bless us, and it makes Him sad when we decide not to follow Him. Which will you choose?

Dear God,

I want to make good choices, but I don't always know what's right. Help me to follow You and obey Your Word, the Bible.

Curses!

The Lord your God would not listen to Balaam.
He turned the curse into a blessing for you.
The Lord your God loves you.

Deuteronomy 23:5 icb

Balaam was a prophet. A king named Barak said he would pay Balaam a lot of money to say bad things about God's special people, the Israelites. Balaam tried to do it, but he just couldn't. He had to say what God told him to say and nothing else. But this was a big problem because he knew it would make King Barak mad.

So three times Balaam went off to talk to God. Each time God told Balaam not to say bad things about the Israelites, but to bless them instead. When Balaam told King Barak that God would bless Israel, the king frowned. "I told you to curse the Israelites, but you keep blessing them!"

Balaam answered, "I can only say what God tells me to say. I cannot disobey God."

Balaam did the right thing to obey God, even though it was hard. Have you ever had to do that? Was it easy or hard? Pray for God to help you be strong enough to do what's right even if you're the only one doing it, like Balaam.

Dear God,

I want to do the right thing. Help me to be strong for You and make good choices even when it's hard.

Sweet Dreams

"Let the one the Lord loves rest safely in him.
The Lord guards him all day long.
The one the Lord loves rests in his arms."

DEUTERONOMY 33:12 NIrV

Do you have trouble sleeping? Sometimes it's hard to close your eyes and slow down after a busy day. Worries may haunt you when you go to bed. Fears like to creep in when it's dark.

Some people count sheep when they can't get to sleep, but I have a better idea. The next time you have trouble falling asleep, think of Jesus, the Good Shepherd, and remember today's Bible verse. *You're* the one the Lord loves, and you can rest safely in Him. He's guarding you all day and all night. Picture yourself sitting in God's lap, snuggling close. His strong arms wrap around you, and your head rests on His chest as He rocks you. Can you hear His big God-heart beating? God is crazy about you! He has promised you His love and protection. He'll give you a safe rest all night long. No need to be afraid.

Psalm 121:3 says, "The LORD is your protector, and he won't go to sleep or let you stumble" (CEV). God stays awake all night to watch over you.

So close your eyes and enjoy a peaceful sleep. God is close. He won't leave your side. Sweet dreams!

Thank You,
God, for being with me while I sleep. Calm my fears and help me to trust in You. Good night.

Loud Horns and Broken Walls

Joshua fell with his face to the ground.
He asked the man, "What message does my Lord have for me?"

JOSHUA 5:14 NIrV

Sometimes when we pray, God tells us to do something. And sometimes what He tells us seems strange. When Joshua and God's people prayed, God told them to do something very strange. But they trusted Him and obeyed Him.

"We need God's help," Joshua said when he saw the great walls around the city of Jericho. Joshua prayed and God spoke to him.

"I want you to capture this city," God said. "The people there will know about Me."

Joshua listened to God's plan. Then he told the people what to do.

"Do what?" the people said.

"God wants us to march around the city," Joshua said. "All the priests should go first and keep blowing their horns. The rest of us will follow. Every day for six days, we will all march around the city once. Don't say a word until I tell you."

Finally on the seventh day, the people marched around Jericho, one, two, three, four, five, six, and seven times. Then the horns blew loud!

Joshua said, "Shout really loud, everyone!"

All the people shouted at once.

Then *crash! Boom! Bang!* The great walls of Jericho fell down flat! God did an impossible thing that no one else could do.

God,

sometimes I don't understand why You want me to do something. But I will just obey. You always know what is right for me. Amen.

"Sun, Stand Still"

Joshua stood before all the people of Israel
and said to the Lord, "Sun, stand still over Gibeon."

JOSHUA 10:12 NCV

Sometimes we need to pray for a miracle when we have something hard to do. Joshua prayed for a miracle in a hard time. Five great kings and their armies were fighting against Joshua's one small army.

Could Joshua's army beat so many soldiers all at once? Joshua stopped right where he was to ask God what he should do. He prayed for a long, long time. God told him, "Go, fight. I will help you."

Joshua sounded the alarm. "Get ready to march!"

Tramp, tramp, tramp! Up the hills and down the valleys, Joshua led his little army. The soldiers went right to where the five great armies were camping. The enemy armies were so surprised that they ran to the mountains.

Joshua's army followed the enemy soldiers into the mountains. They needed to find them, or they would come back to fight again. But it was getting dark!

God knew Joshua's army needed more daylight. So God put an idea into Joshua's mind.

Joshua stood up and said, "Sun, stand still!" The sun stopped moving! It did not go down until all the enemy soldiers were captured. No one had ever seen a miracle like that before—or since.

Dear God,

thank You for giving me a miracle when I must do hard things. Help me to remember that You are always near when I need Your help.

Deborah's Song of Praise

"Let all the people who love you
be as strong as the rising sun!"

JUDGES 5:31 NCV

Praising

God is an important part of praying. Deborah sang a song of praise to God when He helped her people fight against a great army.

Deborah was God's prophet. She told people God's messages. Deborah was also a judge. She sat under a large tree and listened to people who had problems and needed her help.

One day, God gave Deborah a special message. He told her to call for a mighty soldier named Barak. Deborah told him, "God wants you to take your army to Mount Tabor. He is going to help you fight against the great army that is trying to hurt our people."

Barak thought about the great army's strong soldiers and iron chariots. He felt afraid. "Will you go with us?" he asked Deborah.

"I will," said Deborah.

Deborah went with Barak and his soldiers to Mount Tabor, just like God had told them to do.

The great army with its iron chariots and strong soldiers fought against Barak and his men. But God was the strongest. He helped Barak and his men win the battle.

Deborah was so happy that she sang a praise song to God.

Dear God,

thank You so much for loving me and keeping me safe. Help me keep singing praises to You because I love You and want to worship You. Amen.

"Give Me a Sign"

Gideon replied, "If you are pleased with me, give me a special sign. Then I'll know that it's really you talking to me."

JUDGES 6:17 NIrV

If we don't understand what God is saying to us, we need to ask again. In the Bible, God sometimes gave His people special signs. That way, they would know for sure that it was God speaking to them. That is what happened to Gideon.

One day, an angel said to Gideon, "The Lord is with you. Gather together some soldiers because a strong army is coming to fight you."

Gideon wanted to be sure it was God who had spoken. So he prayed, "God, give me a special sign. Tonight, I will lay a piece of wool on the floor. In the morning, if the wool is wet and the floor is dry, I will know You are sending me to fight. I will know that You will help us to win."

The next morning, Gideon hurried to the wool. The wool was so wet that Gideon squeezed out water. He looked at the floor and it was dry.

Again Gideon prayed. "God, don't be angry with me, but I want to be really, really sure. This time, make the wool dry and the floor wet."

The next morning, the wool was dry and the floor was wet.

Now Gideon was ready to obey God.

Dear God,

thank You for the Bible that tells me how You answer prayers. Help me to know in my heart when You are speaking to me. Amen.

Samson Wrestles the Lion

They approached the vineyards of Timnah. Suddenly
a young lion came roaring toward Samson.

JUDGES 14:5 NIrV

A lion is the strongest and most powerful of all the big cats. The lion needs much food to keep him strong. He kills and eats many animals. In Bible days, the lion was a danger to the shepherds who watched their flocks of sheep. Sometimes the lion would hide behind the rocks and bushes along the road, waiting to attack people. One day a lion was waiting to tackle Samson.

Samson was walking down the road with his father and mother. They were on their way to see a young woman Samson wanted as his wife. As they came close to a vineyard, a young lion came roaring out of the bushes.

Grrr-grrr-grrr! roared the lion as it sprang onto Samson. *Grrr-grrr!*

Samson was probably surprised. The lion was strong, but God gave Samson much more power and strength. Samson tore the lion apart with his bare hands. It was so easy for him. God made him strong!

Lions are some of God's strongest creatures. But they're only as strong as God allows them to be. If God wants a man to win a fight with a lion, the lion doesn't have a chance!

God,

You can make a strong person even stronger! Help me to remember that whatever strength I have, I got it from You! Amen.

Honey from the Lion

Some time later, he [Samson] was going back to get married to her. But he turned off the road to look at the lion's dead body. Large numbers of bees and some honey were in it.

JUDGES 14:8 NIrV

Bees are like helicopters! Know why? Because God gave the bee special wings that allow it to fly in any direction—forward, backward, and sideways. A bee also does a little dance to show other bees where to find flowers with nectar. The bees then go bring the nectar back to the colony to be made into honey. Strong man Samson found an unusual place where bees had made honey.

Sometime earlier, a roaring lion had come at Samson. God gave him special powers to tear the lion apart with his bare hands.

Days later, as Samson was going down the same road, he thought about the lion he had killed. So he turned off the road to look at the lion's dead body.

Buzz-zzz! There as a large number of bees swarming around the body. Samson looked into the body and found that the bees had made honey in it. He reached in and dug out some honey with his hands. Mmmm, good. He shared the delicious honey with his mom and dad.

Each honeybee has a special job. The bees all work together to make honey that is not only delicious but good for you. That's bee-utiful!

Dear God,

honey is good! Thank You for the bees that work together to make it. Help me work with others to make or do something good. Amen.

Foxes' Tails Tied Together

So Samson went out and caught three hundred foxes.
He took two foxes at a time, tied their tails together,
and then tied a torch to the tails of each pair of foxes.

JUDGES 15:4 NCV

Foxes are very speedy. Some run as fast as thirty-five to forty miles per hour! Because foxes can run fast, Samson thought of a way to use them against the Philistines—his enemies.

One day, Samson went to visit his wife. The wife's father, a Philistine, would not let him see her. So Samson got very angry with the father and all the Philistines.

"I am going to get even with them," said Samson.

Samson went out and caught three hundred foxes. He took two foxes at a time and tied their tails together. Then he tied a piece of wood on the tails of each pair of foxes. He lit the wood and turned the foxes loose in the fields of grain. The grain belonged to the Philistine farmers.

The foxes burned up all the grain that had been cut and stacked. They burned up all the grain that was still growing. They burned up the vineyards and olive trees. Samson turned the foxes loose because he was angry with the Philistines.

God gives us many things. Whether they are good or bad depends on how we use them. When we use things in anger, it hardly ever turns out good. Remember, the word *anger* is just one letter short of *danger*.

Dear God,
help me to not get angry with others. Help me to love them and try to work things out. Amen.

"...with All His Might."

Samson put his hands on the center pillars of the temple and pushed against them with all his might. "Let me die with the Philistines," he prayed. And the temple crashed down.

JUDGES 16:29–30 NLT

Do you have a favorite superhero? There are so many to choose from—Superman, Batman, Spiderman, and Daredevil are just a few. Samson is not just a superhero. He carried out many heroic acts for Israel's freedom. God's Spirit was with him from beginning to end. He tore a lion apart with his bare hands! He killed a thousand men using a donkey's jawbone! He tore the gates off the city of Gaza! By the power of the Spirit, Samson did many amazing things for Israel.

The greatest thing Samson did was the last thing he ever did. Samson's enemies had captured him and cut out his eyes. He was on display like an animal in a zoo. Had his heroic life ended in defeat?

Samson was taken into a temple to entertain his enemies. Three thousand men and women were watching. He put his hands on the pillars that held the roof of the building. "O God, please strengthen me one more time," Samson prayed. Then God enabled him to push over the pillars, and this destroyed the temple. Thousands of enemies died with Samson that day.

Samson did this to show one last time that God was with him. He died for God's people, and this makes him much more than a superhero. Samson is a hero of the faith.

Dear God,
help me to be a hero
of the faith like Samson.

"Let Me Go Out Into the Fields."

One day Ruth said to Naomi, "Let me go out into the fields to gather leftover grain behind anyone who will let me do it."
RUTH 2:2 NLT

Ruth was very poor. You can see this in the way she got her food. She gleaned behind the reapers—the people who cut grain used to make bread. To glean means to gather up the leftovers. In those days, reapers left some grain at the edges of the fields. Some grain dropped along the way. A gleaner picked up this unwanted grain. Today, some very poor people search through Dumpsters for food that has been thrown away. They could also be called gleaners.

Poor Ruth. She was young and unwanted. Her husband was dead, and she ate what others didn't want. She had only one thing going for her. She had attached herself to Naomi—a child of Israel and a believer in God.

Naomi was the mother of Ruth's husband. There in Israel, she had a relative named Boaz. Ruth happened to be gleaning in Boaz's barley field. Boaz fell in love with Ruth and began to take care of her. This was his blessing to her: "May the Lord, the God of Israel, under whose wings you have come to take refuge, reward you fully."

This blessing comes to people who seek shelter in God.

Dear God,
thank You for blessing people who seek help from You.

"Remember Me"

[Hannah] made a promise, saying, "Lord All-Powerful,
see how sad I am. Remember me and don't forget me. If you
will give me a son, I will give him back to you all his life."

1 SAMUEL 1:11 NCV

Sometimes we make promises to God when we pray. Hannah made a promise—and she kept it. Hannah had been married for a long time, but she had no children. She wanted a child more than anything in the world. One day, Hannah was in the temple praying. The old priest Eli saw her.

He could hear her crying quietly. He saw her lips move as she prayed to God. He could tell that she was very sad.

"What is wrong?" he asked.

"I am sad," answered Hannah. "I have been asking God to help me."

"I will pray for you," said Eli. "May God answer your prayers and give you what you ask." Later, God did answer Hannah's prayers. She had a baby boy and named him Samuel. Baby Samuel grew and grew.

"I must keep my promise to God," said Hannah. She took Samuel to the temple and showed him to Eli.

"Do you remember the day I was here praying?" she asked. "I wanted God to give me a child. Now here he is! It's time to keep my promise. Samuel will be here in the temple to help you whenever you need him."

Hannah praised God for remembering her prayer.

God, thank You for answering my prayers. Help me not to make promises that I cannot keep, and help me keep the promises I do make. Amen.

"Speak to Me, Lord"

Samuel said, "Speak, for your servant is listening."

1 SAMUEL 3:10 NIV

Praying

Praying isn't always talking to God. Sometimes we need to be quiet and listen. Young Samuel learned to listen to God.

Samuel yawned and stretched his arms. He was sleepy, so he lay down and closed his eyes. Then something strange happened. Samuel heard someone call.

"Samuel! Samuel!"

He jumped out of bed and ran to where Eli, the priest, slept. "You called me, and here I am," Samuel said.

Eli looked surprised. "I did not call you," he said. "Go back to bed."

Samuel went back to bed. Everything was quiet. Then he heard the voice again.

"Samuel! Samuel!"

Samuel hurried to Eli. "Here I am. Did you call me?" he asked.

"No," said Eli. "I did not call you. Go back to bed."

Samuel was just closing his eyes when he heard the voice again.

"Samuel! Samuel!"

He ran to Eli for the third time. "Here I am. Did you call me?"

Then Eli knew God was calling Samuel. "When you hear the voice again," Eli told Samuel, "say, 'Speak to me, God. I am listening.'"

Soon Samuel heard the voice again.

"Samuel! Samuel!"

Samuel said, "Speak to me, God. I am listening."

Then something wonderful happened. God spoke to Samuel. And Samuel listened carefully to all God told him.

Dear God,

thank You for listening to the things I want to tell You. Help me to be quiet and listen to the things You want to tell me.

Amen.

"Don't Stop Praying"

They said to Samuel, "Don't stop praying
to the Lord our God for us!"

1 SAMUEL 7:8 NCV

We can pray when people try to hurt us. The people asked Samuel to keep praying when their enemy tried to fight them. God answered Samuel's prayer.

Samuel told the people of Israel to worship and serve God. But they did not listen to him. They did not obey God. Because of this, a great army came to fight with them.

Samuel was sad. He told the people, "God wants you to obey Him. Begin to worship and serve God. He will save you from great armies like this one!"

This time the people listened to Samuel. They got together in the city to pray and worship God.

The leaders of the great army saw them in the middle of the town. They told the army to move forward and fight against them.

The people were afraid. They said to Samuel, "Don't stop praying for God to help us. Keep praying." Samuel prayed that God would help them fight and win.

Bang! Crash! God made a loud clap of thunder. It scared the great army, and the soldiers ran away. The people of Israel knew God had helped them.

Dear God

in heaven, thank You for keeping me safe. When someone wants to hurt me, help me remember to pray. Help me worship and obey You. Amen.

The Sheep, Lion, and Bear

But David said to Saul, "I've been taking care of
my father's sheep. Sometimes a lion or a bear would
come and carry off a sheep from the flock."

1 SAMUEL 17:34 NIrV

Lions can run up to fifty miles per hour! Bears are a little slower. They can run about thirty miles per hour. Both animals are a lot faster than we are! When a lion or a bear is hungry, it can attack another animal and make a fast getaway. So it was important for shepherds to keep a sharp eye on their sheep.

David watched his father's sheep. He would make sure the sheep had plenty of grass to eat and water to drink. He made sure no harm would come to them.

One day while David watched the sheep, a bear charged the flock. It grabbed a sheep and carried it away. David raced after the bear and struck it with his shepherd's staff. The bear rushed toward David, but he was not afraid. He knew God would protect him. He grabbed the bear by its hair, struck it, and killed it.

Another day, a lion sneaked up on the sheep. It grabbed a sheep and took off. David raced after the lion and took the sheep out of its mouth. The hungry lion dashed after David. With God's help, David grabbed the lion and killed it.

Bears and lions can be very fierce when hungry, but God protected David and his sheep, just like He protects us.

Dear God,

thank You for helping us when we are in danger. With You by our side, we have the best protection ever. Amen.

Extraordinary

So tell my servant David, "The Lord who rules over all says, 'I took you away from the grasslands. That's where you were taking care of your father's sheep and goats. I made you ruler over my people Israel. I have been with you everywhere you have gone. . . . Now I will make you famous. Your name will be just as respected as the names of the most important people on earth.'"

2 Samuel 7:8–9 niriv

David of the Bible was once just a kid with chores to do just like you. He was no one special. One of his chores was watching his dad's sheep. He might have wanted to play, but instead he watched the sheep.

David grew into the teenager who killed the giant Goliath. Later, he became king of Israel. God made a special promise to David that He would make him famous and that his name would be known all over the world. That sounds pretty important! God promised this because David loved God very much. God saw David trying to do the right things and obeying his parents and God as he grew up. He did his chores and tried not to complain. God told David He had been with him everywhere he'd been—from the pastures where he cared for the sheep to the king's palace. God took an ordinary kid and helped him become an extraordinary giant slayer and king!

Maybe you feel ordinary now, but God has great plans for you, too. He will be with you wherever you go, just as He was for David. I wonder what God will do for you?

God,

help me to do my chores without complaining. I want to grow up to be someone important in Your eyes, like David. Please be with me wherever I go.

A Promise Is Forever

[God said to David,] And thine house and thy kingdom
shall be established for ever before thee:
thy throne shall be established for ever.

2 SAMUEL 7:16 KJV

When David was a little boy, he was a lot like all little boys. He helped his family take care of their animals. He liked to play with rocks, and he practiced throwing them at targets. He enjoyed music, and he often sang songs to God.

God liked David, and He thought David would make a good king. He promised David that he would be king one day. But it was a long time before that promise came true. While he was waiting, David might have wondered if God was ever going to keep His promise. But God always keeps His promises, and one day, David became the king.

God promised David that his kingdom would last forever. But it was a long, long time before God made that promise come true. Long after David's death, David's great-great-great (many greats) grandson was born. That baby's name was Jesus. He was in David's family, but He was also God's Son. Through Jesus, God kept His promise to David. Jesus was the King, and He is still the King today. His kingdom will last forever.

God has made promises to us, too. He promises to never leave us. He promises to love us and care for us. And He promises that, if we believe in Jesus, we will spend eternity with Him in heaven. At times, we may wonder if God is going to keep His promises to us. But we never have to wonder about that. God kept His promises to David, and He will keep His promises to us.

Dear Father,

thank You for all the promises You gave us. Thank You for always keeping Your promises.

Getting Even

"May the Lord bless you for what you have done.
You have shown a lot of good sense. . . . You have kept
me from using my own hands to get even."

1 Samuel 25:33 NIrV

King David and his men had been traveling a long time. On this trip, they had to pass through land belonging to a man named Nabal. They hoped he would be kind to them and give them some food and water. After all, David had been kind to Nabal as he traveled through his land.

But Nabal was mean and wouldn't help David and his men. One of this mean man's messengers ran to Nabal's wife, Abigail, and told her, "Nabal refused to help King David!" The messenger was afraid David would kill his master. Abigail quickly took lots of food and drinks to the king and told him how sorry she was for the way her husband acted. She told David, "Don't do anything wrong as long as you live" (1 Samuel 25:28 NIrv). She encouraged him to do what would please God.

David thanked her for keeping him from trying to get even with Nabal. He knew God would deal with Nabal's bad behavior.

Do people sometimes make you mad? Do you want to get even with them or hurt them back? God wants us to be kind and loving. Leave the getting even to Him.

God,
sometimes I get so angry that I want to hurt people. Help me to be kind and to leave the getting even to You.

When God Says "No"

"Lord and King, how great you are!
There isn't anyone like you.
There isn't any God but you."

2 SAMUEL 7:22 NIrV

God doesn't always give us everything we pray for. Sometimes He says "No," just like He did to King David.

After David became king, he dreamed of building a beautiful temple. David wanted a place where God's people could gather to worship Him.

God was glad about King David's idea. He told David just how the temple should be built. He told him to get everything ready for the builders. God even told King David what the people could do to help. They gathered wood, stone, and cloth to use in the beautiful temple.

Then God told King David something else. "I have not chosen you to build the temple. I have chosen your son Solomon to build it."

King David could have been sad and upset that he would not be the one to build the beautiful temple. But instead, he was thankful that God had chosen Solomon. He was thankful that the people would have a wonderful place to worship God.

King David prayed a prayer of thanksgiving. "Thank You so much for blessing me and for blessing Your people. You are great, O God. There is no one else like You."

Thank You,

God, for not giving me everything I ask for. You know what I need much better than I do. Help me to be thankful when You say "No." Amen.

"Give Me Wisdom"

"Give me wisdom and knowledge,
that I may lead this people."

2 CHRONICLES 1:10 NIV

Sometimes we ask God for things like a shiny bicycle, a pretty doll, or some new clothes. Solomon didn't ask God for things. He only wanted God to make him wise.

When Solomon became king, he prayed for God to help him. "Give me wisdom and knowledge, that I may lead the people," he prayed.

The people were happy because they knew King Solomon worshipped God. And he was wise enough to know what the people needed. One of the first things King Solomon did was help the people build the temple. It was a grand church where they could worship God.

All the people worked on the temple. *Bang, bang!* Hammers hit the stone. *Zzzz, zzzz!* Saws cut the wood. It took a long, long time.

Finally, the temple was finished. It was very, very beautiful.

King Solomon planned a special party to thank God for the temple. When the people arrived, King Solomon got down on his knees and held his hands up toward heaven.

King Solomon began to pray to God. "There is no other God like You in heaven or on earth," he said. He thanked God for making him wise and for giving God's people such a beautiful place to worship.

Dear God,

thank You for all the things You have given me. Help me to pray for Your help when I have choices to make. Help me to be wise. Amen.

Solomon Rides a Mule

He [David] said to them, "Take my officials with you.
Put my son Solomon on my own mule.
Take him down to the Gihon spring."

1 KINGS 1:33 NIrV

A mule has two different parents. Its father is a donkey, and its mother is a horse. It has a short thick head, long ears, and short mane like a donkey. It is tall and has a shiny coat like a horse. Mules are used for riding and carrying very heavy things. King David rode on a mule and ordered his son Solomon to ride on a mule to be anointed as king.

Because King David was getting old, a new king was needed. King David had promised that his son Solomon would be the next king.

King David ordered the prophet Nathan, "Put my son Solomon on my mule, and take him to the Gihon spring," he said. "Have the priest anoint him as king over Israel. Then bring him back here."

So Nathan put Solomon on the mule and took him to the Gihon spring. The priest took an animal horn that was filled with oil. He anointed Solomon with the oil.

When the trumpet blew, the people shouted, "May King Solomon live for a long time!" The people were happy because they knew King Solomon would make good laws.

God created the mule to be sure-footed so it could carry baggage and people—even a king—through rough land.

Dear God,
thank You for our leaders. Help them be sure-footed, make good decisions, and do good things. Amen.

"The Queen of Sheba..."

When the queen of Sheba realized how wise Solomon was,
and when she saw the palace he had built, she was breathless.

1 KINGS 10:4–5 NLT

The queen of Sheba was from a faraway land. There she heard of Solomon, the king of Israel, and his wisdom. She came to see him and test him with hard questions. Picture this beautiful woman riding into Jerusalem with a long camel train. The camels carried rare spices, gold, and precious stones as gifts for the king. The queen talked with Solomon about everything on her mind. Solomon answered all her questions.

The queen of Sheba saw Solomon's wisdom. She said to him, "What I heard about you was true. You have great wisdom. I didn't believe it until I came and saw it with my own eyes. Your wisdom is greater than what I was told."

Where did Solomon get his wisdom? He asked God for it. "Give me an understanding mind so that I can govern your people well and know the difference between right and wrong," he prayed.

Anyone can have wisdom. All you need to do is ask for it. The Bible says, "If you need wisdom—if you want to know what God wants you to do—ask him, and he will gladly tell you."

Dear God, help me to remember that all wisdom comes from You.

Baboons and Apes

King Solomon also had many trading ships at sea,
along with Hiram's ships. Every three years the ships returned,
bringing back gold, silver, ivory, apes, and baboons.

1 KINGS 10:22 NCV

Baboons and apes are very smart. They can remember lots of things and like to be with people. Many people keep them for pets. King Solomon had baboons and apes in his palace.

King Solomon was very rich. He had a lot of gold. His throne was made of ivory and gold. His cups were made of gold. All the things used in the palace were made of gold.

King Solomon had many ships that would travel to different countries. His ships would bring gold, silver, and ivory to him. Sometimes the ships would bring unusual things such as baboons and apes.

The Bible does not tell what King Solomon did with the baboons and apes. Perhaps he just wanted something different than other kings.

King Solomon was richer than all the other kings on earth. Everyone who came to see King Solomon would bring a gift such as silver, gold, robes, weapons, spices, horses, and mules. King Solomon was very, very wise. He made good decisions for other people but not for himself. Even though Solomon had many things, he turned away from God.

Thank You,

God, for the things You have given me. Help me share with others. Don't let the things I have keep me away from You. Amen.

Ravens Feed Elijah

"You will drink water from the brook.
I have ordered some ravens to feed you there."

1 Kings 17:4 NIrV

Ravens are very wise and can solve many problems. Because these birds have a good memory, God used ravens to help Elijah. God knew they could take food to Elijah. The ravens showed Elijah how much God cared for him.

King Ahab was a bad king. He would not let the people worship God. God sent Elijah to talk to Ahab.

"I serve God, King Ahab," said Elijah, "but you do not obey Him. God told me the rain would stop."

With no rain, the land became dry, and the crops would not grow. God told Elijah that He would take care of him. He showed Elijah where to go.

"Stay and drink from the stream. I have told the ravens to bring you food," said God. Elijah obeyed God.

Caw, caw, caw! The ravens took care of Elijah. God had the birds bring Elijah bread and meat every morning. The birds brought bread and meat every evening. Elijah drank water from the stream.

Elijah obeyed God. He knew that God would take care of him.

Just like Elijah, God will take care of you. And He doesn't need ravens to do so!

Dear God,
thank You for the food I eat and the water I drink. I know You will always take care of me.
Amen.

The Bull on the Altar

"Get two bulls for us. Let Baal's prophets choose one for themselves, and let them cut it into pieces and put it on the wood but not set fire to it. I will prepare the other bull and put it on the wood but not set fire to it."

1 KINGS 18:23 NIV

In Bible times, a bull was used as a sacrifice on the altar when people worshipped God. Elijah used a bull to help the people understand about God's power.

King Ahab had led the people to pray to a false god named Baal. Elijah asked the king's prophets to have a contest with him to see which god was the most powerful—the god Baal or Elijah's God.

"Put a bull on the altar," Elijah told the prophets. "Now pray to your god Baal and ask him to bring fire down to the sacrifice."

So the prophets prayed to their god. "Baal! Answer us!" they prayed, but Baal did not answer.

Elijah laughed at the prophets. "Maybe Baal did not hear you," he said. "Call louder." So the prophets called louder, but their god did not hear them.

Then Elijah called the people to his altar. He placed a bull on it. "Pour water around the altar of stones, on the wood and bull," said Elijah. "Do this three times." Then he prayed to God. God heard his prayer and sent fire on the sacrifice. The stones, wood, and sacrifice burned down to ashes. Then the people worshipped Elijah's God.

God is all-powerful. He can do anything and everything.

Dear God,
You are powerful and can do mighty things. You are my God. Help me to always worship You and no other god. Amen.

Keep Praying

[Elijah] bent down toward the ground.
Then he put his face between his knees.
1 KINGS 18:42 NIrV

Sometimes God answers our prayers quickly, and sometimes we must keep praying. Elijah had to keep praying for a long, long time before God answered his prayer.

The ground was dry. There was no green grass. The rivers had no water. Not a drop of rain fell!

One day, God told Elijah, "I will send rain."

Elijah and his helper climbed to the top of a mountain. Elijah bowed his head and talked to God.

After Elijah prayed, he told his helper, "Go and look toward the ocean. See if there are any clouds."

The helper ran to look. "I don't see any clouds," he said.

Elijah prayed again. The helper looked toward the ocean—but still no clouds.

Elijah prayed again. He asked his helper to look two, three, four, five, six more times. But still there were no clouds. Elijah kept praying.

"Go look one more time," said Elijah.

This time, Elijah's helper saw something—about the size of a man's hand. Could it be a cloud? Yes! It was a small cloud!

The cloud grew bigger and bigger. The sky became dark and the winds blew. *Pitter-patter, pitter-patter!* The rain fell on the dry ground. God finally answered Elijah's prayer.

Thank You,

God, for sending rain to make the world beautiful and provide water for the animals to drink. Help me to keep praying for things I need, just like Elijah did. Amen.

Elisha Plows with Oxen

Then Elisha left his oxen.
He ran after Elijah.

1 KINGS 19:20 NIrV

Oxen are much stronger than horses. In Bible times, oxen were used for plowing the fields as well as pulling heavy loads. Most of the time, two or four pairs of oxen would do the work needed for each job. Oxen were very important animals.

God told Elijah that he needed a helper. As Elijah walked along, he saw Elisha plowing in his fields. Elisha was plowing with twelve pairs of oxen—that means twenty-four oxen. That's a lot of oxen!

Elijah went up to Elisha and threw his coat on him—which meant for Elisha to follow him. Elisha left his oxen and ran after Elijah.

"Let me go tell my father and mother good-bye," said Elisha. "Then I'll come with you."

"Go back," said Elijah.

Elisha went back, got two oxen, and killed them. He burned the plow to cook the meat of the oxen. He gave the meat to the people and they ate. Then Elisha started to follow Elijah. He became Elijah's helper.

Oxen are usually used in pairs. Two oxen joined by a yoke can double the work of one. After leaving his farmwork and oxen behind, Elisha was yoked with Elijah in a new job. Together they taught many people how to be prophets.

Lord,
I want to follow You. Show me what job You would like me to do. Tell me who You want me to work with. Amen.

The Bear Attack

Elisha turned around, looked at them, and put a curse on them in the name of the Lord. Then two mother bears came out of the woods and tore forty-two of the boys to pieces.

2 KINGS 2:24 NCV

A bear can run very fast—much faster than a human. A bear has strong muscles so it can dig roots and bugs out of the ground to eat. The strong muscles help the bear to climb trees and tear apart its enemies. One day God sent two strong bears to help Elisha.

Elisha had just left Jericho. There he had done a miracle. Elisha made the water in the spring pure so the people could drink it again. Now he was walking down the road out of the city.

Suddenly some boys came out of the town and started making fun of Elisha.

"Go up, you baldhead!" they yelled again and again.

Elisha turned around and looked at the boys. Then he put a curse on them in the name of the Lord.

Suddenly two mother bears came out of the woods. They attacked forty-two of the boys. They no longer bothered Elisha.

God does not like us to mock people who are different than we are. A good rule is this: if you can't say anything nice about someone, don't say anything at all. And if anyone makes fun of you, ask God to bless him or her. It may not change the mocker, but it will make you feel better. And it will please God.

Dear God,

help me to not make fun of others. And if anyone makes fun of me, help me forgive, and then ignore them. Amen.

Behind Closed Doors

Elisha went into the room. He shut the door.
He was alone with the boy. He prayed to the Lord.

2 KINGS 4:33 NIrV

Many times we pray with other people—like at home or church. But sometimes God wants us to pray alone, just like Elisha did.

Elisha traveled around telling people about God. Many times, Elisha visited a man and woman who had no children. Since Elisha came to the city often, the couple built a room for him to stay in. Because of their kindness toward Elisha, God blessed the couple with a son.

One day, while the son was in the field with his father, he became very sick.

His father brought him to the house. His mother carried him into Elisha's room and laid him on the bed. Then she hurried to find Elisha.

When Elisha saw the woman coming, he knew something was wrong. Immediately, they hurried back to the house. Elisha went into the room and closed the door. He was alone with the boy. Then he prayed.

Elisha lay on the bed with the boy. Then he walked back and forth across the room. Suddenly the boy sneezed one, two, three, four, five, six, seven times, and opened his eyes. The boy's parents were very happy. Elisha's prayers had been answered.

Dear God,
thank You for letting me pray with others. But help me to remember that You also would like to have some time alone with me. Amen.

"He Suffered from Leprosy."

But though Naaman was a mighty warrior,
he suffered from leprosy.

2 KINGS 5:1 NLT

This man Naaman was powerful and desperate. He was the commander of the Syrian army. He was also a leper. This means he suffered from an incurable disease of the skin called leprosy. Naaman heard of a prophet in Israel who could cure him. So he went to Israel to find Elisha the prophet. When he found him, he was told to wash in the Jordan River seven times. This made Naaman furious.

Naaman was an important man! He'd come to Israel with all his followers carrying hundreds of pounds of silver and gold. He arrived at Elisha's poor little house expecting more than he got. Naaman expected Elisha to come out of his house. But Elisha's servant came out instead. Naaman wanted Elisha to say some magic words. He expected a sacrifice to God and some soothing ointment for the leprosy. Instead, he was told to wash in the ordinary water of the Jordan River. Naaman was too proud to do this.

The same is true today. People are sick in their souls. They don't have leprosy, but they have sin. And they are too proud for the simple remedy of faith. This cure seems too simple. But it is God's way. Faith in Jesus is the only cure for sin.

Dear God,
help me not
to be prideful.

"Deliver Us"

"Now, O Lord our God, deliver us from his hand,
so that all kingdoms on earth may know that you alone,
O Lord, are God."

2 KINGS 19:19 NIV

When someone wants to hurt us, we can ask God to keep us safe. When Hezekiah got a letter saying a great army was coming to destroy his land, he prayed and asked God to keep his people safe.

Hezekiah was a good king. He loved and respected God, and he told his people to worship God, too. God blessed him. Hezekiah and his army began to win all their battles. Each time they won a battle, Hezekiah would thank God for helping them.

One day Hezekiah got a letter from Sennacherib, a king from another country. Sennacherib said he and his army were strong and would destroy Hezekiah and his army. He said that God would not help Hezekiah.

When Hezekiah got the letter, he went to the temple and spread the letter out in front of him. He prayed to God.

"You are the only God," said Hezekiah. "We are in trouble. Sennacherib has a strong army. We need help. Save us from the powerful Sennacherib. Show him and his soldiers that You are the only God."

God heard Hezekiah's prayer and took care of the great army for them.

Dear God

in heaven, thank You for keeping me safe when someone wants to hurt me. Help me remember that You can help me when I am in trouble. Amen.

"Enlarge My Territory"

Bless me.

Jabez cried out to the God of Israel,
"Oh, that you would bless me and enlarge my territory!"
1 CHRONICLES 4:10 NIV

Sometimes we say long prayers and sometimes we say short prayers. Jabez said a very short prayer. But it was a powerful prayer.

When Jabez was young, he heard about God. He heard how God rescued His people from great armies and placed them in a land He had promised them. Jabez knew that God would hear him, even if he prayed a short prayer.

Jabez asked God to bless him. He knew God wanted to give him many good things, but he also knew he had to ask for them.

Jabez asked God to "enlarge his territory." This meant that he wanted to tell more people about God.

Jabez knew he needed God to be near him at all times. Sometimes things were hard for him, and he needed God to help him. He asked God to give him kind words to say and to help him do right things.

Then he asked God to keep him away from the bad things that might hurt him.

When he prayed for these things, God answered him and gave him the things he wanted. God blessed Jabez's friends and family— all because Jabez wanted to please God in all he did and said.

Dear God,

help me pray like Jabez. Bless me every day. Help me tell people about You. Be near me at all times and keep bad things away from me. Amen.

"We Trust in You"

Asa called out to the Lord his God. He said, "Lord, there isn't anyone like you. You help the weak against the strong. Lord our God, help us. We trust in you."

2 CHRONICLES 14:11 NIrV

We can pray and trust God because He knows what is best for us. King Asa trusted in God because he knew that God would always help him.

When Asa became king, he saw that the people had not been worshipping God. They had disobeyed God's laws. King Asa knew that God was not pleased.

The king told the people they must worship God. He ordered them to obey God's laws. He told the people to trust God because God knew what was best for them.

Another king who lived in a nearby country did not want Asa's people to worship God. So King Asa knew he needed to gather an army of men. Some of the soldiers carried spears. Some carried bows and arrows. All of the men were very brave.

Finally the day came for the bad king and his soldiers to fight King Asa's army. King Asa knew he needed God's help to win the fight.

King Asa prayed, "Lord God, there is no one like You. We are weak but we know You can make us strong. So Lord God, help us. We trust in You. You are our God."

God heard King Asa's prayer. His soldiers won the fight.

Dear God,

I'm so glad that You always know what is best for me. Help me to trust in You when I feel very small and weak. Amen.

The Battle Is the Lord's

"O our God, will you not judge them?
For we have no power to face this vast army that is attacking us.
We do not know what to do, but our eyes are upon you."

2 CHRONICLES 20:12 NIV

We can pray when we don't know what to do. Then we can do what Jehoshaphat did after he prayed—stand back and let God take care of things.

As soon as Jehoshaphat heard that the enemy army was coming, he was afraid. He knew he didn't have an army big enough to win the battle.

But Jehoshaphat had something bigger than an army. He had God, who could do anything. So he decided to ask God what he should do.

All the people came together to pray for God's help. They came from all the towns around. Jehoshaphat stood up among the people.

"Lord, You are the God of our people," he prayed. "The enemy is coming, and we don't have the power to face this huge army. We do not know what to do, but we know You can help us."

One of the men standing nearby said, "King Jehoshaphat, listen! God has spoken to me. Do not be afraid. The battle is God's. He will take care of the great army."

The next day, Jehoshaphat and his men found that God had won the battle for them. Jehoshaphat and his men sang praises to God for answered prayers.

Dear God,
sometimes I don't know what to do. Help me remember to pray and then stand back and let You take care of things. Amen.

A Safe Trip

We [gave up eating] and prayed to our God about our trip,
and he answered our prayers.

EZRA 8:23 NCV

We can pray for a safe trip whether we walk, ride our bikes, travel in a car, or fly in an airplane. Ezra and his people prayed for God to keep them safe on their trip.

A crowd of people stood by the river. They were packed and ready to go home. Ezra was the wise man who would show them the way.

"I could have asked the king for soldiers to guard us," Ezra told the people. "But I told the king that God would keep us safe. We will ask God to guard us. When we get home safely, it will show the king and the people that God takes care of those who love Him."

The next morning, before they left for home, the people gathered together to pray. They prayed during the day as they walked. They prayed as they rested at night.

Day after day, they traveled. Sometimes they saw robbers hiding by the road, but God kept them safe. After many weeks, they finally reached their homes. God had answered their prayers. He kept them safe on their trip!

The next time your family goes on a trip, ask God to keep you all safe.

Dear God,

I thank You for loving me and taking care of me. Thank You for keeping me safe at all times— no matter where I go. Amen.

"Grant Me Favor"

"Give your servant success today
by granting him favor."

Nehemiah 1:11 niv

We can pray when we are sad. Nehemiah prayed when he was sad, and God heard his prayer.

Nehemiah was a special helper to the king. He lived in a country far from his home and family. In those days, people would build strong walls around their towns. The walls kept out all kinds of dangers—fires, floods, wild animals, even big armies.

One day, Nehemiah's brother told him some sad news. "The walls of the city where we used to live are broken down. The city is not safe."

Nehemiah was sad. So Nehemiah prayed to God.

When the king saw Nehemiah, he asked, "Why are you sad?"

"I am sad because the wall around the city where I used to live is broken down," Nehemiah answered. "I would like to go and help rebuild the wall around my town."

The king told Nehemiah, "You can go and help build the wall."

When Nehemiah came to the city, he met with the people. "We can work together to build the wall," he said. "We will make it strong again."

Bang, bang! Hammers and chisels cut the stone. *Zzzzz, zzzzz!* Saws cut the wood.

Soon the walls were fixed and the city was safe. God had heard Nehemiah's prayer.

Dear God,

thank You for always hearing my prayer. Help me remember to pray when I am sad. Help me to remember that You can make me happy again.
Amen.

"Why Is This Happening to Me?"

Job replied to the Lord,
"I know that you can do anything.
No one can keep you from doing what you plan to do."

JOB 42:1–2 NIrV

When we are having a bad day and everything seems to be going wrong, we can pray. Job had many bad days, but he kept on trusting God.

Did you have a bad day? Perhaps you fell and scraped your knee. Or you didn't get to go with your friends to the park. Maybe you didn't feel good. Some days are just like that!

Job obeyed God, and God gave him many things—a big family, a lot of land, many animals. God even kept Job from being sick. Job loved God and always did what was right.

One day, everything seemed to go wrong for Job. He lost his family and his animals. He got sick. Job didn't know why these things were happening.

"You must have done something wrong," said one of his friends.

"I have done nothing wrong," answered Job. "I love God and serve Him."

Then Job asked God, "Why is this happening to me?"

"Don't I know what is best for you?" answered God.

Then God did something that surprised Job and his friends. God made Job well. Then He gave him back everything he had lost—and much, much more.

Job trusted God even when things were going wrong!

Dear God,

You know what is best for me. Help me trust in You when I'm having a bad day and things go wrong. I love You, God.

Amen.

"...a Shield Around Me."

So many are saying, "God will never rescue him!"
But you, O Lord, are a shield around me, my glory,
and the one who lifts my head high.

PSALM 3:2–3 NLT

This is a song by David, the king of Israel. At the time, his own son, Absalom, was hunting him down. Absalom rebelled against his father. He even tried to kill him and take over the throne of Israel.

Things were so bad for David that people said not even God could help him. But nothing is impossible for God. He can always help. David found help in God, and so can we.

David said, "O Lord, You are my shield and my glory, the one who lifts my head high." He prayed, crying out loud to the Lord, and he knew that God heard him. His faith made him sure of this. What great hope we have that God hears our prayers!

Prayer gave David real peace. This is why he tells of how soundly he could sleep, despite his troubles. "I lay down and slept," he said. "I woke up in safety, for the Lord was watching over me." David made his requests known to God, and his heart and mind were kept by God's peace.

Dear God,
please give me the same peace King David had by trusting in You.

"Hear Me When I Call"

The Lord will hear when I call to him.

PSALM 4:3 NIV

God wants us to pray whenever we need His help. God chose David to be the new king—but even kings need help sometimes. He prayed that God would protect him and God answered his prayer.

Many people wanted to be king. Some people were jealous and angry when God chose David, especially old King Saul. He didn't want a young shepherd boy to take his place as king. He tried to kill David many times, but God kept David safe.

King Saul's men chased David, but God always showed David where to hide.

David hid from King Saul in the desert. David hid in the hills. The old king and his men searched for him every day. But they could never find David.

One night, King Saul and his men were sleeping in a cave. They were tired. They had been chasing David all day long. David came quietly into the cave. He tiptoed over to where the king was sleeping. David could have killed Saul. But he knew God didn't want him to hurt the king.

Finally, King Saul died. David became king, just as God had planned.

What can you do when you are in trouble? You can pray to God and know that He will help you.

Dear God,

thank You for helping me when I'm in trouble. Thank You for keeping me safe just like You did for David. Amen.

Never Alone

Those who know the Lord trust him.
He will not leave those who come to him.
PSALM 9:10 ICB

When are you most afraid or lonely? Maybe it's when you go to a new place or at night when you're in bed. Most people, even grown-ups, feel lonely and scared sometimes, and that's okay. It's perfectly natural to feel that way.

But here's the good news—no matter how alone or afraid you feel, Someone is always with you. This Someone loves you very much and will always take good care of you. You can trust this Someone even more than your mom or dad! Can you guess who it is? It's God!

Our verse today says, "Those who know the Lord trust him." Do you know God? If you often feel afraid, try to get to know Him better. How do you get to know your friends? By spending time with them and talking to them, right? You can do the same thing with God by reading your Bible and talking to Him through prayer.

Our verse also says that God won't leave those who come to Him. So when you need a friend, talk to God. He'll stay right by your side and never, ever leave. Now that's a friend you'll want to keep forever!

God,
I want You to be my forever friend. Help me to trust You so I'm not afraid or lonely. Thank You for always staying with me.

Fort God

The Lord is my rock and my fort. He is the One who saves me.
My God is my rock. I go to him for safety.

PSALM 18:2 NIrV

Have you ever built a fort? What was it made of? Snow? Blankets and chairs? What's the coolest thing about being inside a fort? Sometimes forts are given names like Fort McHenry or Fort Knox. What would you name your fort?

The Bible talks about a fort, too. But this fort is better than any we could build. Our verse today says, "The Lord is my rock and my fort. He is the One who saves me. My God is my rock. I go to him for safety."

When you hold a rock in your hand and squeeze it hard, what happens? Does it squish? No, it stays strong and doesn't change. That's how God is! And because He's so strong, He can keep us safe.

During wartime, soldiers hide inside their forts or even fight from them. Forts are their place of safety. They protect them and save them from danger. That's what God does for us, too. He protects us and gives us a safe place to hide when we're afraid. So the next time you're scared, run to Fort God. He will save you and protect you.

Thank You,

God, for being my strong, safe place. Help me remember to run to You when I am afraid.

"...the Glory of God."

The heavens tell of the glory of God. The skies display his marvelous craftsmanship. Day after day they continue to speak; night after night they make him known.

PSALM 19:1–2 NLT

Do you want to know God? Is there someone you love who you hope will believe in God? Here is an easy way to see God. The heavens announce God's glory. The skies shout about the work of His hands.

This has been happening since the fourth day of Creation, when God said, "Let bright lights appear in the sky." Since then, they continue to speak about God day after day. Night after night, they make Him known. If only people would pay attention! It doesn't matter where you are from or what language you speak. Nature tells all about God. Yes, God is invisible. But the Bible says that God and all of His power can be seen through nature.

Many people pray that their family and friends will be open to God. They want them to believe in Jesus Christ. We hope they will hear the Gospel. God's Creation is the greatest preacher of all. Let's pray that everyone will see it and believe it!

Dear God,

help me to open
my eyes every day
to see Your
wonderful Creation.

Tender and Kind

A father is tender and kind to his children. In the same way, the Lord is tender and kind to those who have respect for him.

PSALM 103:13 NIrV

Think about a time you had a bad day and felt sad. Maybe you went to your mom or dad to talk about it. What did you hope your mom or dad would do? Maybe hug you close and let you cry. Or whisper, "I love you and everything will be all right." You probably wanted someone to be kind and tender to you.

Your mom and dad sometimes have a bad day, too. They may be too tired to listen as much as you'd like. Maybe they're busy doing things like making supper or mowing the lawn. But even if it seems they don't have enough time for you, they always wish they did. They love you very much.

Whether your parents do what you hope for on those days or not, you can always count on God to listen to you. He's never in a hurry or too busy to hear what's bothering you. God is always kind to anyone who respects Him. And He can always help you with your problems.

So talk to your parents whenever you can. But don't forget to talk to God, too. He's always there for you.

Thank You,

God, for being so kind and gentle to me. I know You care and will always listen when I talk to You.

Love You Forever

But the Lord's love for those who fear him continues forever and ever. And his goodness continues to their grandchildren.

PSALM 103:17 ICB

How long is forever? It's so long that it's hard to explain! It never ends. It goes on and on and on. . .more times than we can say "and on." What do you wish would last forever?

There *is* something that goes on forever. It's God's love for you. Think about that for a minute. God loves you when you praise Him. He loves you when you're at school or day care. He loves you when you're at home or at Grandma's house. God loves you when you're sad and when you're sick. He loves you when you're silly. He loves you when you're kind. He loves you when you're mad, when you're young, and when you're old. God even loves you when you disobey.

Is there ever a place or time God doesn't love you? No! Even after you die, God's love will live on in your children and grandchildren. God's love is humongous! You can be thankful that He loves you no matter what. He could never love you any more or less than He already does. Doesn't that make you want to love God right back? Well, go ahead! Blow Him a kiss!

God,
I'm glad You love me forever, on good days or bad. I'll love You forever, too. Help me to show You how much.

Do Right

Blessed are those who always do what is fair.
Blessed are those who keep doing what is right.

PSALM 106:3 NIrV

It's important to be fair to others. Nobody likes someone who cheats or is dishonest. That makes God sad.

Sometimes your friends might do something you know isn't right or fair. What should you do? It takes a lot of courage to tell them what they did wasn't right. You might suggest another way of doing things. You shouldn't go along with your friends if you know they're doing something wrong.

Our verse says blessed, or happy, are those who "do what is fair" and "keep doing what is right." You may have to choose to do what is right over and over again. You should do the right thing as many times as you have the chance. Even grown-ups have to choose to do the right thing again and again. Galatians 6:9 says, "We must not become tired of doing good. We will receive our harvest of eternal life at the right time. We must not give up!" (ICB).

So keep practicing doing what's right while you're young so you'll be really good at it by the time you're all grown up. Eternal life is worth working for. Don't give up!

God,

I want to live a happy life by being fair and doing what is right. Help me not to get tired of doing good.

Food for Thought

He provides food for those who have respect for him.
He remembers his covenant forever.

Psalm 111:5 NIrV

Have you ever heard your parents worrying about how they'll be able to pay their bills? Or maybe you asked for something at the store and they said, "No, we don't have enough money."

There are a lot of things we want—but only a few things that we really *need*. We need food and water. We need a place to live. We need clothes. Most of all, we need Jesus to take our sins away.

Our verse today promises that God will give food to those who respect Him. It doesn't say the food will be your favorite meal, complete with ice cream for dessert. But He always gives us just enough food for each day. It might be vegetables. It could be steak! Or it might be pizza or a peanut butter and jelly sandwich.

Our verse says God remembers His covenant forever. A covenant is a promise. He'll always remember to give you food if you remember to respect Him. Respect is to look up to someone or to honor them. One way you can do that is by thanking Him for whatever food He gives you today—whether you like it or not!

Thank You, God, for all the different kinds of food You give us. I wish they all tasted as good as. . .But even if they don't, thank You anyway!

Forever and Ever

Lord, your word is everlasting.
It continues forever in heaven.

Psalm 119:89 ICB

Everlasting

is a long time. It's forever! You know how it seems to take a really long time for Christmas or your birthday to come each year? Everlasting is a lot more than a million times longer than that. But when you're talking about something *good* lasting that long instead of having to wait for something, it's wonderful!

God's Word, the Bible, is everlasting. Unlike your favorite shirt or pajamas, you'll never outgrow the things it teaches. The Bible is true, and it can always help you no matter how young you are now or how old you'll be later. Our verse says God's Word "continues forever in heaven." That means it's not going anywhere, and it isn't going to change just because we do. What it says is true, both now and when you grow up.

That's a good, solid foundation to build your life on! Read your Bible and do what it says. You can count on God's Word to lead you in the right direction forever, no matter what happens to you. It's trustworthy and true, just like God.

God,

sometimes I don't feel like reading Your Word. Help me to want to read my Bible and spend time with You.

A Parent's Joy

Children are a gift from the Lord. They are a reward from him. . . .
Blessed are those who have many children.

PSALM 127:3, 5 NIRV

The day you were born was one of the happiest days of your parents' lives. They probably have pictures of you when you were a baby. You may have been crying in some of them. Or maybe your parents were feeding you, giving you a bath, or just holding you so you'd feel loved. They did important things to help you grow up healthy and happy.

But did you know you do important things for your parents, too? You give them great joy just by being their child. They love to hear you laugh. It makes them proud when you learn something new. And most of all, when you follow God by obeying your parents and being kind, they can almost burst with happiness!

The Bible says children are a gift from God. You may not fit in a box with wrapping paper and a bow on top, but you're probably the best present your parents ever got. Give them an extra-special hug tonight and tell them how much you love them. Then watch the joy spread across their faces.

Dear God,

thank You for my parents.
I love them. Help me to
make them happy just
by being myself.

Clear Path

With all your heart you must trust the Lord and not
your own judgment. Always let him lead you,
and he will clear the road for you to follow.

PROVERBS 3:5–6 CEV

Have you ever tried to do something your own way but it ended up a big mess? Maybe your parents even told you to do it differently, but you wouldn't listen. It's hard to give up our own way and do things someone else's way. But when God says in His Word you should do something a certain way, you should listen and obey.

God always wants what's best for us. He wants to help us win. And God never makes mistakes. That's why we can trust whatever He says.

Have you ever gone hiking and the trail got kind of rocky and hard to walk on? Our verse today tells us that if we let God lead us, He'll clear the rocks off the trail so it's easier to follow Him. He wants our path to be smooth so we don't trip and get hurt.

Sometimes we don't follow God. We take a different path. But this way is always harder to walk because God only smoothes out *His* path for us. So save yourself a lot of stubbed toes and skinned knees and stay on God's trail. You can trust Him to lead you.

God,
I hate stubbing my toe.
So thanks for clearing
the rocks off my path.
Help me to trust You and
stay on Your path.

The Wise Ants

Go watch the ants, you lazy person.
Watch what they do and be wise.

PROVERBS 6:6 NCV

A tiny ant is very strong! Depending on its species, an ant can lift and carry things that are three to twenty-five times its own weight! That is like you lifting three to twenty-five other kids your own size. That's strong! Ants live in colonies, much like a town. They depend on one another and help each other when they have a job to do. Working together, ants can find answers to hard problems.

In Bible times, wise men wrote many things that helped people make good choices. Solomon, a wise man, used the ant to show people how important it was to work together to get a job done well.

Solomon told lazy people to watch the ant. The ant goes out and looks for food. When it finds something, it lifts it and carries it back to its home. If something is too heavy for an ant to carry home, he calls other ants to come help. The ants store up food in their home so they will have something to eat when food is scarce.

We need to be wise like the ant—to work together to get things done. We also should always be prepared to help others—just like our friend, the ant.

Thank You,
God, for the wise ant.
Make me strong. Help me
to work with other people
to get things done well.
Amen.

Remember

My son, keep your father's commands. Don't forget your mother's teaching. Remember their words forever. Let it be as if they were tied around your neck. They will guide you when you walk. They will guard you while you sleep. They will speak to you when you are awake.

PROVERBS 6:20–22 ICB

How is your memory? Do you remember songs from TV commercials? Do you find it easy to retell jokes you've heard? How about the things your parents teach you about what's right and what's wrong? Do you remember them?

In our Bibles, Solomon was the wisest man ever. He knew that parents always want the very best for their children. That's why they teach you right from wrong. They don't want you to get into trouble or hurt yourself. They want you to follow God's ways because they know it will bring you the best life possible.

Have you ever worn a scarf around your neck in the winter? Were you warmer and more comfortable? Solomon said you should wear your parents' teaching around your neck like a scarf. You'll be more comfortable when you let their lessons wrap around you. You'll feel warm inside as you listen to their voices reminding you to make good choices. When you remember what they said, doing the right thing will become easier to do.

Work on remembering what your parents say. Follow their rules even when they're not around. You'll feel as snug and warm as when you wear your favorite scarf.

God,
thank You for my parents. Sometimes I forget what they teach me. Help me to listen carefully to them so I can live my best for You.

Wise Guy

A wise child brings joy to a father.

PROVERBS 10:1 NLT

What makes your parents really happy? Playing golf? Watching a movie? Reading a book? The Bible tells us what brings your mom and dad the greatest joy. It's you!

When you make good choices and live the way God tells you to in His Word, it makes your parents' day. Think about it. What happens when you make bad choices? You get in trouble or you might even find yourself in a dangerous situation, right? Your parents want you to be happy and safe. It's no fun when you get punished. And your parents don't like to punish you when you disobey either. But they know they have to so you'll grow into the boy or girl God wants you to be.

If you obey and choose to do the right thing, your parents won't have to be sad about correcting you. They'll be happy because you made a wise choice and so will you!

So be a wise guy. Make your dad and mom's day by obeying the first time. Good choices make everyone glad!

God,
I want to be wise and make my parents glad. But most of all I want to make You happy. Help me to listen and obey.

"I'm Rich!"

People who do what is right will have rich blessings.

PROVERBS 10:6 ICB

You know it's best to do what's right. But why is it best? Just to keep you out of trouble? Because it makes your mom and dad happy? Those are good reasons, but there's another one you may not have thought of.

Our verse today says, "People who do what is right will have rich blessings." Remember who gives us blessings? God does! Doing what's right makes God happy, and that's even better than making your mom and dad happy. If you please God by doing the right things and making good choices, you won't just receive regular old blessings. You'll receive *rich* blessings! God's blessings are often things we can't see or touch like love, peace, joy, and hope. And you can't buy them. They're things that are too good to put a price tag on. We could never have enough money to pay for blessings like that. But you'll be rich with blessings from God!

So do what is right and receive God's rich blessings. And it's nice to stay out of trouble and keep your mom and dad happy, too!

God,

help me to make good
choices. I want to please
You and stay out of
trouble, too. Thank You
for giving me rich blessings.

The Rich Life

The blessing of the Lord brings wealth.
Trouble doesn't come with it.

PROVERBS 10:22 NIrV

What does it mean to be wealthy? It means being rich. Wealth usually means a lot of money. Our verse says, "The blessing of the Lord brings wealth." Does that mean everyone who loves Jesus will have lots of money? No. They'll have something even better.

God's blessings are better than all the money in the world. They help us enjoy life in ways that money can't. Money can't buy everything. It can only buy things. But God's blessing of love helps us feel special, because we know we belong to Someone special. When things aren't going very well and we're having problems, God's blessing of peace helps us to not feel so afraid. And when we feel as if we're going to burst with happiness, God's joy bubbles up and makes us happier than we ever thought possible.

Knowing that Jesus is coming back to save us from the troubles of this world gives us hope, another one of God's amazing blessings. And God's blessings don't bring any trouble with them. Only good things.

So enjoy the rich life God's blessings bring. You'll be richer than the wealthiest man in the world.

God,
I'm thankful that You give us blessings that are better than money. Help me to remember to look for Your blessings every day.

"Here Am I. Send Me!"

I heard the voice of the Lord saying, "Whom shall I send? And who will go for us?" And I said, "Here am I. Send me!"

ISAIAH 6:8 NIV

God can talk to us when we pray. When God talks, He wants us to answer quickly. Isaiah was ready to answer when he heard God's voice.

Isaiah lived in a city where people were doing bad things. People had turned away from God. They were lying and stealing. They were saying things that were not pleasing to God. They did not worship God.

One day while Isaiah was worshipping in the temple, he heard God's voice say, "Whom shall I send to speak to these bad people?"

"Here am I. Send me!" said Isaiah.

God was pleased with Isaiah for answering Him quickly. God told Isaiah to go and tell the people to stop doing bad things. "Tell them to obey Me and do what is right," said God.

For many years, Isaiah asked the people to stop doing bad things and obey God. Isaiah warned the people what would happen if they kept disobeying. But only a few listened.

Isaiah was sad that the people did not want to obey and worship God.

But he was glad he had answered God's voice. He was doing what God had asked him to do.

Thank You,
God, that I can talk to You and hear what You want to tell me. Help me to always do what You ask me to do. Amen.

Awesome God

Thank You, Jesus!

Lord, you are my God. I honor you and praise you. You have done amazing things. You have always done what you said you would. You have done what you planned long ago.

Isaiah 25:1 ICB

What are some of the things you like most about God? When you tell God or other people those things, you're honoring Him and praising Him just as our verse says. Living in a way that makes God happy is another way to honor and praise Him.

Isn't it neat we can say that God is ours? We can say, "Lord, You are my God," just as Isaiah did. God has enough love for all of us to share and still have plenty to go around. He's ours, and we're His.

Our verse says God has done amazing things. Can you think of something amazing God has done?

God had a plan even before He made the world, and that plan included you! He knew people would make mistakes and sin, so He planned right from the beginning that He would send Jesus to die for our sins. He did that so we could live together with Him forever. That means you, too! God always does what He says He will do. He did what He planned long ago, and He still keeps His promises today.

What an awesome God!

Thank You, God, for always keeping Your promises. Help me to honor and praise You in all that I do.

Invisible Teacher

"All your children will be taught by the Lord.
And they will have much peace."

ISAIAH 54:13 ICB

Do you have a favorite teacher? It could be a teacher at school, your Sunday school teacher, or even your mom or dad. The Bible talks about a teacher we all have but have never seen. Can you guess who it is?

It's God! The Bible book of Isaiah says, "All your children will be taught by the Lord. And they will have much peace." Everyone starts out as a child. So we are all taught by God.

How can we learn from an invisible teacher? God teaches us through the Bible. It's His instruction manual for how we should live. When we listen to His Word and do what it teaches, we'll have a happier life. That doesn't mean nothing bad will ever happen to us. But if something bad does happen, God will help us get through it. We won't have to be so afraid. That's what His peace does for those who trust Him.

So don't forget to be a good listener to the teachers you can see and especially to the One you can't!

Dear God,

I want to be a good student who learns from You. Help me to do what Your Word says.

"...Watchmen on Your Walls."

O Jerusalem, I have posted watchmen on your walls; they will pray to the Lord day and night for the fulfillment of his promises. Take no rest, all you who pray. Give the Lord no rest until he makes Jerusalem the object of praise throughout the earth.

Isaiah 62:6–7 NLT

Policemen watch over our towns and cities. They try to make sure that nothing bad happens to us. In ancient Israel, policemen were called watchmen—because the time between sunset and sunrise was divided into three watches. Each watch had different watchmen, so someone had to stay up all night to watch the city and keep it safe from enemies.

The Bible says that God has set watchmen on the walls of Jerusalem. These are not the actual watchmen who kept an eye on Jerusalem—they are Christians who pray. Wouldn't you like to be a watchman like that? They don't shout that enemies are coming—they pray to God until He makes Jerusalem a thing of praise in the earth. That happens when Jesus comes back.

We don't have to be strong or famous to pray like this. Small prayers are important prayers. A person who says to God, "Lord, I love You," has said something very important. Someone who can stop and say, "Thank You," to God has done something very special. You could be that person!

Dear God,

help me to thank You in prayer every day!

Mind Reader

"I will provide for their needs before they ask.
I will help them while they are still asking for help."
Isaiah 65:24 icb

Have you ever hurt yourself and run crying to your parents? Mom or Dad may have had a hard time understanding what was wrong because you couldn't stop crying long enough to speak. Unless you were bleeding, no one could tell why you were so upset. Maybe you were asked to show where it hurt.

Your parents love you and hate to see you hurting or sad. God is the same way. He wants to make you feel better, just like your mom and dad. But there's something different about God. He knows what's wrong even *before* you come crying to Him. And by the time you settle down enough to tell Him, He's already getting you the help you need. That's because God sees everything that happens to you and knows how you feel about it. He's always with you and can read your mind!

So the next time you run to your mom or dad in tears, remember that God is already busy working on the answer to your problem. He'll help you before you even have time to ask, because He loves you very much.

God,

thanks for always being with me and knowing just what I need. I trust You to take care of everything when I get hurt.

"I'm Only a Child"

"You are my Lord and King," [Jeremiah] said.
"I don't know how to speak. I'm only a child."

JEREMIAH 1:6 NIrV

Do you think you are too young to tell people about God? Then ask God to help you, just like Jeremiah did. He thought he was too young to speak to people about God, too.

The people God loved had forgotten Him. They no longer worshipped Him. God needed someone to take a message to His people.

One day, God spoke to young Jeremiah. "I want you to take My message to the people," said God. "Before you were born, I planned for you to speak for Me."

"But I'm so young," said Jeremiah. "I don't know how to speak to people."

"Don't worry about that," God said to Jeremiah. "I'll tell you exactly what to say. There's no reason to be afraid."

Then God touched Jeremiah's mouth. God said, "Now you are ready. Just listen, and I will tell you just what to say."

Jeremiah got ready to tell the people God's message.

God spoke to Jeremiah again. "Do as I tell you. The people may not like what you tell them, but remember that I am with you. I will keep you safe."

Dear God,

I know that I am young, but I can tell someone about You. Help me to be brave and speak the words You want me to say. Amen.

"Call Me"

"Call to me and I will answer you. I'll tell you marvelous and wondrous things that you could never figure out on your own."
JEREMIAH 33:3 MSG

Did you ever wake up from a bad dream and call for your mom or dad? Maybe you had to call two or three times before one of them heard you. When your parents came, how did you feel? Did they help you understand that your dream wasn't real and you didn't have to be afraid?

As great as a parent is when you call out, God is even better. He hears you the first time you call and comes running. He whispers in your ear things you never knew, things only God knows. He reminds you that you're safe with Him.

He'll help you understand things you can't work out without His help. Like how to handle that bully at school, or how to be polite when you're blamed for something you didn't do. God will help you figure things out when you have no idea what to do. You can trust what He tells you because He loves you and always wants what's best for you.

So go ahead and call out to God. Listen for His thundering footsteps and then His soft whisper in your ear. He's got all the right answers.

God, sometimes I forget to call out to You when I need help. Remind me that You're there and want to help me. I'll trust You and listen to You.

Showers of Blessing

"I will send down rain at the right time.
There will be showers of blessing."
EZEKIEL 34:26 NIrV

I saw a movie once where it rained gumballs. If you could make it rain something besides water, what would you choose? Gummy bears? Ice cream cones? Money? They wouldn't be as good as God's rain.

God makes a wonderful promise to us in today's verse. He promises to send rain at just the right time. And not just any kind of rain—showers of blessing! What do you think that means? Remember that a blessing is something good that happens or that someone gives you.

Wouldn't it be wonderful if God rained blessings down on us? Really, He already has. Look around you. Everything you see is a blessing from God—your toys, your family, the Bible, trees, flowers, friends, animals, the sun and moon. But sometimes blessings are things we can't see like love, joy, peace, and knowing Jesus. What blessing would you like God to rain down on you and your family?

Our verse says He'll send *showers* of blessing. Not just a little drizzle or sprinkle, but a downpour! God loves to bless His people. So put up your umbrella and get ready for rain!

God,
I like to run in the rain. Help me to enjoy Your showers of blessing as much as I love getting wet. Thank You for blessing me.

One, Two, Three Times

Three times each day Daniel would kneel down to
pray and thank God, just as he always had done.

DANIEL 6:10 NCV

God hears us every time we pray. Daniel prayed—one, two, three times—every day, and God heard his prayer each time.

The king gave Daniel an important job. But some men did not like Daniel. They were jealous. They thought of a plan to get Daniel in trouble.

The men told the king, "Let's make a new rule. Everyone must pray to you." The king thought this rule was a good idea. He told the people they must pray only to him.

The next day, Daniel prayed to God—one, two, three times—just as he always did. The men, who were watching Daniel, ran to tell the king what they had seen.

The king was sad he had made the new rule. The men had tricked him. Now he had to throw Daniel into the lions' cage for disobeying the new rule.

The lions went r-r-roar! They were very hungry. R-r-roar!

But Daniel was not afraid. He knew God would take care of him.

The next morning the king came to the lions' cage. Daniel called out, "King, I am safe. God took care of me! He sent an angel to shut the lions' mouths."

The king made a new rule. Everyone should pray only to God.

Heavenly Father,

help me to remember to pray when I'm afraid. Keep me safe when I'm in trouble. Thank You for hearing my prayer every time I pray. Amen.

Jonah and the Big Fish

The Lord caused a big fish to swallow Jonah, and Jonah
was inside the fish three days and three nights.

JONAH 1:17 NCV

Fish come in many sizes, shapes, and colors. The biggest fish in the world today is the whale shark. This gentle giant is bigger than a school bus! One time God made a fish big enough to swallow a man. The man's name was Jonah.

God told Jonah to go to Nineveh and tell the people about God. Jonah did not want to go, so he got on a ship going the other way.

Who-oo-oo! The winds blew. The ship was tossed about. The sailors were afraid.

The ship captain yelled at Jonah, "Why are you asleep? Get up and pray for God to help us!"

Jonah told the men, "I'm the reason for the storm. I ran away from God. Throw me into the sea and it will be calm."

The men threw Jonah into the sea. A big fish swallowed Jonah. *Gulp!* It was dark and smelly in the fish's belly.

"I am sorry for disobeying," prayed Jonah. "I will do what You want me to do, God."

Ugh! God caused the fish to throw up Jonah. Then Jonah went to Nineveh.

This story does not tell us what kind of big fish swallowed Jonah. But it does teach us that we can't run away from God. And it's always best to do what He wants us to do.

Dear God,

let me know what You want me to do. Then help me do it. Amen.

Jonah and the Little Worm

Before sunrise the next day, God sent a worm.
It chewed the vine so much that it dried up.

JONAH 4:7 NIrV

Worms are slimy. They have between one to five hearts! And if a worm is cut into two pieces, only the part of the body that has the head will live. One day a worm spelled trouble for Jonah.

After the big fish threw up Jonah, he obeyed God and traveled to Nineveh. There he told the people that God was going to destroy them because they were doing bad things. The people were afraid. They prayed to God with all their hearts. They said they would no longer do bad things. So God did not destroy them.

This made Jonah mad. He said to God, "I knew You might do something like this. That's why I didn't want to come in the first place!" Then Jonah sat down outside the city.

It was hot. So God made a vine grow beside Jonah to give him shade. This made Jonah very happy. Then before sunrise the next day, God made a worm to eat the vine. The worm ate so much that the vine dried up. Then God sent a hot wind and a burning sun. Jonah got mad again.

God told him, "You care more about this vine than you did about the people of Nineveh!"

Do you care more about other people than your own comfort?

Dear God,
help me to love other people more than I love the things I have. Amen.

"Safe!"

The Lord is good. When people are in trouble, they can go to
him for safety. He takes good care of those who trust in him.

NAHUM 1:7 NIrV

When you play tag, sometimes there's a "base" that makes you safe. When you reach that base, no one can tag you or get you out. If someone's chasing you, and you make it to the base in time, you yell, "Safe!" so they know they can't tag you. Then they have to find someone else to chase.

Today's verse says there's a safe place to go when we're in trouble, just as there's a safe place to go in tag. When we run to God by praying to Him and telling Him what's wrong, He becomes our safe place. Our verse says the Lord is good, and He takes good care of those who trust in Him. It's hard to trust in a God we can't see, but He's the only One powerful enough to help us. He can do anything! Jeremiah 32:17 says, "Oh, Lord God, you made the skies and the earth. You made them with your very great power. There is nothing too wonderful for you to do" (ICB).

So when you're in trouble, run to God. He's more powerful than anything you can imagine. And He loves to be a safe place for His children.

God,

I feel safe when I talk to You. Thank You for listening when I tell You my troubles and for being powerful enough to help.

"...a Ruler of Israel."

But you, O Bethlehem Ephrathah, are only a small village
in Judah. Yet a ruler of Israel will come from you.

Micah 5:2 nlt

Bethlehem was a tiny place. Why do you think Jesus was born there? The name Bethlehem means "the house of bread." Jesus is the Bread of Life. It was in the little town of Bethlehem that the Bread of Life came to us. That is when Bethlehem became the real house of bread.

The Bible also calls Jesus the Good Shepherd of the sheep, and we are His sheep. It's interesting that He was born in Bethlehem because it was the town of David. David was a shepherd, too, and later he became the king of Israel.

The night that Jesus was born, shepherds were in the fields outside of Bethlehem. They were guarding their sheep. Suddenly, an angel of the Lord appeared, and they were very afraid. But the angel said, "Don't be afraid! I bring you good news of great joy! The Savior has been born tonight in Bethlehem! Go there and you will find a baby wrapped up and lying in a manger."

Those shepherds went into Bethlehem, the town of King David. There they found Jesus, the Good Shepherd. He was sleeping in a manger. A manger is the place where farmers put food for their sheep and cattle. The Good Shepherd is also spiritual food for His sheep—and we are His sheep!

Dear God,

thank You for sending Jesus to give His sheep the spiritual "food" they need.

Frightened!

You shall bear a son.

And the angel said unto her, Fear not, Mary: for thou hast found favour with God. And, behold, thou shalt conceive in thy womb, and bring forth a son, and shalt call his name Jesus.

LUKE 1:30–31 KJV

One night, a young girl named Mary was sleeping. Suddenly, a loud voice woke her up! She opened her eyes to a bright light, and she didn't know what was happening. Mary covered her face, wanting to hide from whatever was in her room.

But peeking through her fingers, she saw a beautiful creature all in white.

"Greetings, Mary!" said the angel, whose name was Gabriel. "Don't be afraid. God thinks you are really special. He wants you to be the mother of His Son. You will name Him, 'Jesus.'"

Mary was afraid, and didn't know what to think. She had never seen an angel before. Maybe she wanted to cry, or tell the angel to go away. Maybe she wanted to run away herself! But she didn't. She loved God, and she was willing to do whatever God wanted her to do.

God had a plan to bless Mary, and He wanted to bless the whole world through her. Even though she was frightened, she chose to obey God.

Dear Father,

I thank You for sending Jesus. I'm glad Mary obeyed You, even though she was afraid. When I feel afraid, help me to remember that You love me and that I am special to You.

New Dad

But while he thought on these things, behold, the angel of the Lord appeared unto him in a dream, saying, Joseph, thou son of David, fear not to take unto thee Mary thy wife: for that which is conceived in her is of the Holy Ghost. And she shall bring forth a son, and thou shalt call his name Jesus: for he shall save his people from their sins.

MATTHEW 1:20–21 KJV

Joseph was surprised to learn that Mary was going to have a baby. At first, he wasn't sure if he wanted to adopt her son or not. One night, while he was trying to figure out what to do, he had a dream.

In this dream, an angel spoke to him. The angel said, "Joseph, don't be afraid to make Mary your wife and adopt her son. He is God's Son, but He will need a dad here on earth. His name will be Jesus, and He will be a blessing to the whole world."

Joseph obeyed God and adopted Jesus. He became Jesus' dad, and he was proud of his son. Sometimes, when we're not sure what to do, we can just wait. If we ask God to help us, He will show us what He wants us to do.

Dear Father,

sometimes I don't know what to do. Help me to always look to You for answers. I know that You will help me to do the right thing. Thank You for leading me in the way I should go.

Choosing a Name

For unto us a child is born, unto us a son is given: and the government shall be upon his shoulder: and his name shall be called Wonderful, Counsellor, The mighty God, The everlasting Father, The Prince of Peace.

Isaiah 9:6 KJV

Before a baby is born, that baby's parents spend a lot of time choosing a name for their child. A name is important, for it will stay with that child throughout life. Often, the parents will choose a name that reflects a positive character trait. Or perhaps they will name their child after someone they admire.

When Jesus was born, He was given many names. Each name tells us something about who He is. He is called Wonderful because He is wonderful. He is called Counselor because He helps us to make good choices.

Jesus is the Mighty God. He is not beneath God—He is God! He is the Everlasting Father. Even those who don't have a father here on earth can claim Jesus as their Father. He will never stop being Father to all who ask.

He is the Prince of Peace. Even when things are scary and unsettled, we can know peace if we know Jesus.

Jesus has many more names, as well. Each name tells us how great He is. Each one lets us know how much He loves us.

Dear Father,

thank You for giving Jesus many names, so we could know more about Him. Help me to know and remember all the wonderful things about Him.

God with Us

Now all this was done, that it might be fulfilled which was
spoken of the Lord by the prophet, saying, Behold, a virgin shall
be with child, and shall bring forth a son, and they shall call
his name Emmanuel, which being interpreted is, God with us.

MATTHEW 1:22–23 KJV

God had promised His people that His Son was coming to be their king. For a long, long time, they had looked forward to Jesus' arrival. They had waited and hoped and prayed. It had been so long, some of them wondered if it was ever going to happen!

But God gave them signs to look for, so they would know Jesus was really God's Son. They were to look for a young girl who was going to have a baby. She would name her son, "Immanuel," which means, "God with us." When those things happened, they would know that God had kept His promise.

When Jesus was born, God truly did come to live with us. Instead of being in heaven where no one could see Him, He became a man. People could now talk to God and touch God and hug God and laugh with God. Because Jesus is God, the people were able to be with Him. When Jesus came, God was really with us!

Jesus was with the people when He was born. Today, God is still with us, watching over us and caring for us. He is all around us, and we can talk to Him any time. He promises to never, ever leave us.

Dear Father,

thank You for choosing to be with us. I know I can talk to You any time, and You will never leave me.

Good Citizens

And it came to pass in those days, that there went out a decree
from Caesar Augustus that all the world should be taxed. . . .
And all went to be taxed, every one into his own city.

LUKE 2:1, 3 KJV

Caesar Augustus was the emperor of the Roman Empire. He wanted to know how many people lived in his kingdom. Every few years, he made all the people go to their hometowns so they could be counted.

At that time, travelers packed up enough belongings for a long trip. The people who still lived in their hometowns didn't have far to go. But if anyone had moved away, he or she had to pack food and water and clothes to last for many days. They didn't have cars or trains or airplanes back then. Most of the people had to walk to their hometowns. A few people rode donkeys.

When they got to their hometowns, they registered and told how many people were in their families. This way, Caesar would know how many people lived in his kingdom. He used this information for all sorts of things. It helped him know how many taxes to collect, how many guards to hire, how many roads to build, and other things.

It is important for us to do what our government asks us to do, as long as they don't ask us to disobey God. Governments help countries and kingdoms run more smoothly. God wants us to obey the laws and be good citizens.

Dear Father,

thank You for placing people in charge of my government who want to help take care of me. Please give them wisdom as they work to try and make my home a good and safe place to live.

Trust and Obey

And Joseph also went up from Galilee, out of the city of Nazareth, into Judaea, unto the city of David, which is called Bethlehem; (because he was of the house and lineage of David:) to be taxed with Mary his espoused wife, being great with child.

Luke 2:4–5 KJV

Mary and Joseph's families had moved away from their hometown, a place called Bethlehem. Now they lived in the town of Nazareth. Mary and Joseph had to pack up their things and make the long journey back to Bethlehem, so they could be counted. They wanted to be good citizens, so they obeyed their emperor.

It was close to time for Mary to give birth to Jesus, but that didn't matter. She still had to go to Bethlehem to be counted. It was probably a difficult journey for her. She may have wondered why God would ask her to do such a hard thing. But she didn't fuss or complain. She did what she was asked to do. She trusted that God had a reason for making her take that long trip.

Dear Father,

sometimes I have to do things I don't want to do. At times, I have to work when I'd rather play, or I have to go to sleep when I want to stay awake. Sometimes I have to take long trips, and sitting in the car for hours isn't fun. Help me to have a sweet attitude. Help me to trust You, even when I don't understand.

No Room

There was no room for them in the inn.

LUKE 2:7 KJV

Bethlehem was very crowded. Everyone in all the surrounding towns had walked or ridden their donkeys to Bethlehem so they could be counted. Only the first people there were able to find hotel rooms. The others had to sleep outside on the ground. Some of them may have slept in tents.

Joseph wanted Mary to have a warm place to stay. He knew the baby would be born soon, and he didn't want the baby to be born in the cold, windy night air. "Please, sir, can you find a place for us?" he asked the busy innkeeper. He knew how crowded it was, but he was hoping that someone would see that Mary was going to have a baby soon and make room for her.

The kind innkeeper looked at Mary. He wanted to help, but all his rooms were taken! He couldn't kick out any of his customers. After all, they were there first. He didn't know what to do.

Then, he had an idea. "Come with me," he said. "You can stay in my stable. At least it's warm there." He led them to where he kept his animals. It smelled of hay, and the animals probably made noises.

"*Baaaa!*" said the sheep.

"*Mooooo!*" said the cow.

Joseph led Mary into the warm stable. He made her comfortable in the hay and thanked God for taking care of his family.

Dear Father,

thank You for always taking care of us. Even when things don't go exactly as we planned, we know You are watching over us.

It's Time!

And so it was, that, while they were there, the days were
accomplished that she should be delivered.

LUKE 2:6 KJV

Joseph and Mary made themselves comfortable in the soft hay of the stable. They may have made friends with the animals there, talking to them and giving them names. Perhaps Mary's own donkey stayed in the stable with them.

Before long, Mary looked at Joseph. "I think it's time," she told him. It was time for Jesus to be born. Since this was their first child, Mary may have felt afraid. Perhaps there was a woman nearby—maybe the innkeeper's wife—who had been through this before. Perhaps she helped Mary to stay calm.

Joseph may have helped, too, or he may have paced back and forth nervously, praying that his wife and the baby would be okay. But he didn't need to worry. The baby who was about to be born was God's Son. God would take care of them.

God's Son, Jesus, was the King of Kings. God could have chosen for His Son to be born anywhere. He could have been born in a huge mansion or a palace. But He wasn't born in any fancy place. He was born in a stable, surrounded by hay and animals. God chose for Jesus to be born in a place where anybody and everybody could find Him.

Dear Father,

thank You for sending Your Son as a gift to the world. You didn't hide Him from us, or make it difficult for us to find Him. You promised that everyone who looks for Him will find Him. Thank You for Jesus.

The Gift in the Manger

She. . .wrapped him in swaddling clothes, and laid him in a manger; because there was no room for them in the inn.

LUKE 2:7 KJV

Chomp, chomp, chomp. The donkeys crunched on the hay filling the manger.

"Baaaa!" A sheep nudged his way in, claiming some of the meal for himself.

Little did the animals know, later that night their feeding trough would hold a great treasure.

When Jesus was born, Mary needed a soft place to lay Him. Because they were in a stable, there were no fancy cradles. She didn't want to lay Him on the ground—He might get stepped on!

"Here, honey. We can lay Jesus in this manger," Joseph may have said. The hay provided a soft cushion, and it kept Him safe from animals' hooves.

Who would have thought that the King of Kings would make His bed in a smelly old feeding trough? This proves that you cannot judge a gift by its package. After all, Jesus was God's most precious gift to the world. And God didn't choose to wrap Him in an expensive, sparkly package. Instead, Jesus was wrapped in simple cloths, and He slept in a manger.

Sometimes, the best gifts are the ones that come in simple packages. They may lack sparkle, but they are filled with love. Those are the gifts that will last and last, even after the package has been discarded.

Dear Father,

thank You for the gift of Your love. Thank You, also, for the reminder that Your best gifts often come in simple packages.

Doing Their Jobs

And there were in the same country shepherds abiding
in the field, keeping watch over their flock by night.

LUKE 2:8 KJV

A shepherd's job is to take care of sheep. It isn't an easy job, for sheep need to be watched all day and all night long, every single day. If a shepherd doesn't do his job, one of the sheep might wander off and get lost or hurt.

There are many dangers to sheep, especially if they become separated from the rest of the flock. They might fall off a cliff and break a bone. Wolves might attack them. Being a shepherd is a demanding job.

On the night Jesus was born, some shepherds were nearby watching over their flocks. Some of the shepherds may have thought, I'm tired. I don't want to watch over these silly old sheep. Why can't they take care of themselves? I want to go home and go to bed. But we should always do our jobs, even when we don't feel like it. When we obey God and do what we are supposed to do, He blesses us.

Little did those shepherds know that in a stable nearby, the Son of God was being born. If they had stayed home and not done their jobs that night, they might have missed one of the most exciting nights of their lives!

Dear Father,

thank You for blessing me when I obey You. Thank You for giving me important jobs to do. Help me to always do what I'm supposed to do, with a cheerful attitude.

A Bright Light

And, lo, the angel of the Lord came upon them, and the glory of the Lord shone round about them: and they were sore afraid.

LUKE 2:9 KJV

"Baaa, baaa," called the sheep. The shepherds lay on the ground, listening to their flocks and looking up at the stars. Some of them dozed, while others fought to stay awake.

Suddenly, a bright light filled the sky! It lit up the fields and covered the sky as far as they could see.

They placed their arms over their eyes to shield themselves from the bright light. What in the world is happening, they must have wondered. It is the middle of the night! Why is the sky filled with light?

The light they saw was God's glory. God was happy that His Son had been born, and He wanted the whole world to know. An angel was in the middle of the light. The angel was there as God's messenger, sent to announce Jesus' arrival.

The shepherds were afraid, maybe even terrified! They had never seen anything like this before! Was this a dream? Would the winged creature hurt them? But no, the creature didn't seem angry or mean. It seemed to have something important to tell them. Even the sheep seemed amazed, and they grew quiet.

Although the shepherds were confused, they knew this was a very special night. They looked at the angel, listening for some explanation.

Dear Father,

thank You for loving me enough to send Your Son to earth. As I celebrate His birth, help me to be excited about Your love for me.

A Special Night

And the angel said unto them, Fear not: for, behold, I bring you
good tidings of great joy, which shall be to all people.
For unto you is born this day in the city of David a Saviour,
which is Christ the Lord.

LUKE 2:10–11 KJV

The shepherds had never been so terrified in all their lives. They had been coming to these fields every night for years, and nothing like this had ever happened. Bright lights, winged people in the sky, voices in the air. . .it was unbelievable!

Then the angel spoke to them. "Don't be afraid! I have good news. What I'm about to tell you will make you very happy."

The shepherds watched and listened with their mouths hanging open.

The angel continued. "Today in Bethlehem, God's Son has been born!"

What? How could this be? The shepherds had heard that God was sending a Son. Ever since they were small children, they had been taught about God's promise to their people. But could this really be true? Could God's own Son—the One their parents and grandparents and great-grandparents had waited for—could He really have been born this night, just over those hills?

The shepherds looked at one another. They wanted to know if the others had seen and heard the same thing. Some of them may have pinched themselves to see if they were dreaming. If what the angel said was true, this was truly a special night!

Dear Father,
thank You for sending Your angel to tell the shepherds about Jesus. I want to be like that angel, and share Your good news with everyone.

Searching for the King

And this shall be a sign unto you; Ye shall find the babe
wrapped in swaddling clothes, lying in a manger.

LUKE 2:12 KJV

The shepherds were having a hard time believing their own eyes and ears. Bright lights in the sky? Angels? God's Son, born nearby? It was just too amazing to be true.

The angel must have known they needed a sign. "Go see for yourselves!" the angel told them. "Go to Bethlehem and look for Him. You'll find Him wrapped in cloths and lying in an animal's feeding trough."

Again, the shepherds looked at one another. Why, this story was getting crazier and crazier! A feeding trough? A manger? Why on earth would God send His Son, the Prince of Peace, to be born in a stable? Why would God allow the King of Kings to lie in a smelly, dirty manger?

They jumped to their feet and ran to see for themselves, leaving their sheep behind. Over hills they ran, jumping over rocks and small bushes. Good thing God had sent that bright light, so they could see the path!

Into the center of town they ran, darting in and out of stables, not even caring if they woke up the whole city. "Is He here?" they called to one another.

"No, not in this one. Let's try that one over there!"

"Nope. No baby in here."

"Hey, guys! Come over here! I think I've found Him!"

The shepherds followed their friend's voice to the stable. Sure enough, there was a young couple there. And lying in the manger, wrapped in swaddling clothes, was a newborn baby. . .just like the angel said.

Dear Father,
thank You for Jesus.

Angels Everywhere!

And suddenly there was with the angel a multitude of the heavenly host praising God, and saying, Glory to God in the highest, and on earth peace, good will toward men.

LUKE 2:13–14 KJV

The angel sent the shepherds to Bethlehem. He even gave them a sign to look for, so they'd know they had found God's Son. But before the shepherds could even stand up, the sky filled with angels—more angels than they could count!

These angels weren't talking, though. They were singing! It was the most beautiful music the world had ever heard. Their music filled the skies with praises to God for sending His Son to earth.

"Glory to God!" they sang. "Glory to God in the highest, and on earth peace!"

They knew that Jesus would provide the way for people to have peace with God. Jesus would make it possible for people to have their sins forgiven.

"Peace to men on whom His favor rests," the angels continued. They knew that the only reason God would send His Son to earth was because He loved people so much. God knew that the only way people could have peace was through Jesus Christ.

They sang and sang. We should sing, too, and praise Him every day for loving us.

Dear Father,

thank You for loving us so much that You sent Jesus. Thank You for giving me peace. Help me to remember to sing songs to You, out loud and in my heart.

Spreading the Word

And when they had seen it, they made known abroad the saying
which was told them concerning this child.

LUKE 2:17 KJV

The shepherds couldn't believe their eyes. They had searched and searched, and they'd found God's Son lying in a manger, just as the angel had said they would. This was the One they had heard stories about. This was the One they had waited their whole lives for. This was the One their parents and grandparents and great-grandparents had waited for.

After spending a few minutes looking at the baby, they knew they couldn't keep this news to themselves. "Let's go tell everyone," they whispered.

With a respectful bow, they slipped out of the stable. "Thank you for letting us see your baby," they whispered to Mary and Joseph as they left.

As soon as they were outside, they began to walk quickly. Then they began to run. "God's Son is here!" they shouted. "The One we've waited for has been born tonight, right here in Bethlehem! God has kept His promise. The Messiah has come at last!"

People may have stirred from their sleep. "Who is that, waking us up in the middle of the night?" they may have asked.

Some of them arose and went to see for themselves. Others may have pulled the covers over their heads and gone back to sleep. But no matter their response, the shepherds continued to tell everyone they met the good news: Jesus had arrived!

Dear Father,

I want to be like the shepherds, telling everyone I know about Jesus.

The Wise Men

Now when Jesus was born in Bethlehem of Judaea in the days of Herod the king, behold, there came wise men from the east to Jerusalem, saying, Where is he that is born King of the Jews? for we have seen his star in the east, and are come to worship him.

MATTHEW 2:1–2 KJV

"Look at that star!" The man pointed, and his friends looked at the sky. The man and his friends were very smart. They had spent years studying the stars. They believed they could learn things about God by watching His creation.

"Do you think that's the one?" asked another man. "Could that be the star that will lead us to God's Son?"

"Let's go find out," replied the first man. The wise men packed up their belongings and left right away. They didn't care how long it took them. They were ready to travel as far as they needed to, so they could see Jesus. After a long time, they found Jesus and his parents. They knew they were in the presence of God's Son.

The wise men looked for Jesus, and they knew they would find Him. We can look for Jesus, too. Oh, we may not see Him in person. Still, we can look for ways that He shows His love to us. We can look for ways to show His love to other people, for when we show His love, Jesus is there.

Father,

thank You for sending the wise men to Jesus. I want to be wise, too. I want to spend each day seeking Your love and Your plan for my life.

King Herod

When Herod the king had heard these things,
he was troubled, and all Jerusalem with him.
MATTHEW 2:3 KJV

The wise men traveled a long time looking for Jesus. They had to stop to rest and for food and water. When they stopped, they talked to the people who lived in that place. "We're looking for the newborn king," they said excitedly.

One night, they stopped in King Herod's town. When Herod heard the men were looking for the king of the Jews, he was concerned. I'm the king, he thought. Who is this baby they are looking for? He became worried that someone was trying to take his job from him.

Herod wanted to find out who this baby was. He wanted to make the baby and his family go away, so they wouldn't try to take his job. He didn't understand that Jesus' kingdom wasn't here on earth.

Herod pretended to be interested in baby Jesus. He told the men, "When you find the baby, come back and tell me where He is, so I can send Him a present. I want to worship Him, too."

But Herod didn't really want to send a gift. He didn't really want to worship Jesus. He wanted to kill Him.

If Herod had only taken time to find out more about this baby, he would have known that Jesus didn't come to be an earthly king. He came to be the King of our hearts.

Dear Father,
thank You for sending Jesus to be the King of my heart. I want to worship You with my life.

Following the Star

When they had heard the king, they departed; and, lo, the star, which they saw in the east, went before them, till it came and stood over where the young child was. When they saw the star, they rejoiced with exceeding great joy.

MATTHEW 2:9–10 KJV

"There it is. Let's go that way!" one of the wise men called to his friends. "I think we're getting closer."

The wise men traveled for a long time. Night after night, month after month, for more than two years they followed that star! The star kept moving, guiding them to where they needed to be. At times, they probably grew tired. They may have wondered if they would ever reach their destination. Maybe they even thought about turning around and going home.

But they kept going. They didn't give up. Finally, the star stopped over the house where Jesus lived with His parents. They couldn't believe their eyes! Was their journey finally coming to an end?

As the wise men approached the house, they were filled with joy. At last, they would see the One they had searched for! At last, they would meet God's Son, Jesus. They knew this was a very special day, indeed.

The wise men followed the star. They went where God led them, and He gave them joy. When we follow God, He helps us to feel joyful, too.

Dear Father,

I'm glad the wise men followed where You led them. I want to follow You, too.

Gifts for Baby Jesus

And when they were come into the house, they saw the young child with Mary his mother, and fell down, and worshipped him: and when they had opened their treasures, they presented unto him gifts; gold, and frankincense and myrrh.

<small>MATTHEW 2:11 KJV</small>

The wise men could hardly believe their eyes! They had traveled for so long, and at times they had wondered if they would ever reach the new King. But there in front of them was a house. The star they had followed stood still, directly over that house. They knocked on the door, and Mary answered. "May I help you?" she asked.

"We're here to see God's Son. Is He here?"

"Yes, He is." She invited them in. Maybe she offered them something to eat or drink. But no matter how tired and thirsty the men were, they probably had only one thing on their minds. They wanted to see God's Son!

Jesus was about two years old. Perhaps He was eating His lunch, or building with some blocks. The men came right in and knelt down in front of Jesus.

They gave Him gifts, too. The gifts were expensive gifts, suitable for a king. Jesus was too young to understand how nice the gifts were. Mary thanked them and put the gifts away, for when Jesus was older.

We can give Jesus gifts, too. Oh, we may not have fancy gifts like the wise men gave. But the thing Jesus wants most is our hearts. When we love Him with our whole hearts, we give Him the most precious gift of all.

Dear Father,

I love You. Please help me to love You more each day, with my whole heart.

The Greatest Gift

For God so loved the world, that he gave his only begotten Son,
that whosoever believeth in him should not perish,
but have everlasting life.

JOHN 3:16 KJV

Christmas is a fun time, filled with surprises and brightly wrapped gifts. Everywhere we go, we see beautifully decorated wreaths and hear festive music. Christmas brings fun secrets and delicious food. For many people, Christmas is the most wonderful time of the year.

The colorful trees are pretty, but they aren't the reason we celebrate Christmas. The music is nice to listen to, but it's not the reason for Christmas either. The gifts are fun to open, but even they are not the reason we celebrate Christmas. The purpose of the season is not about the gifts we receive on Christmas morning. It's about the gift that God gave a long time ago.

Jesus is the reason we celebrate Christmas. The word *Christmas* actually comes from His name—Christ. We celebrate Christmas because God loved us so much that He sent His Son, Jesus, to live with us. Jesus lived His life for us, so we could see how to live. Then He gave His life for us, to take the punishment for our sins. No matter how great the new bicycles and the dolls and the games and the new puppies may seem, none of those gifts compares to the true gift of Christmas: Jesus Christ.

God gave us a gift, and we can give a gift back to Him. He loves us, and He wants us to love Him, too. When we choose to love Him with our whole hearts, we give Him the perfect gift.

Dear Father,

thank You for giving the greatest gift of all time— Your Son.

"There Is the Lamb of God."

The next day John saw Jesus coming toward him and said, "Look!
There is the Lamb of God who takes away the sin of the world!"

JOHN 1:29 NLT

Everyone knows that Jesus wasn't really a lamb. He was a man. For His whole life, He wasn't like a lamb at all. He was strong and bold until the end. Then He became like a lamb. The Bible says that when Jesus died, "He was led as a lamb to the slaughter. And as a sheep is silent before the shearers, he did not open his mouth."

In the times of the Old Testament, people made sacrifices to God for their sins. These sacrifices were usually lambs. Year after year, people made these sacrifices. Then Jesus came. He was the last sacrifice for sin. No one has to kill a little lamb again because of sin. Jesus is the Lamb of God whose death took away the sin of the world. "For God so loved the world that he gave his only Son, so that everyone who believes in him will not perish but have eternal life."

Dear God,

thank You for giving Jesus to be the sacrifice for my sin.

"I Need Some Men to Help Me"

One of those days Jesus went out to a mountainside to pray,
and spent the night praying to God.

LUKE 6:12 NIV

God wants us to pray whenever we need something. Jesus did that when He asked God to send Him some helpers.

Jesus was tired. He walked up the mountain and found a cool place to sit down and rest. All day, Jesus had been busy helping sick people. He had told many moms and dads about God's love. But still many, many people were sick. More moms and dads needed to know about God's love. Jesus wanted to help every person.

Jesus prayed all night. He asked God to help Him choose twelve special helpers.

The next morning as the bright sun began to warm the earth, Jesus knew what God wanted Him to do. He called all His friends together.

"I need some men to help Me," Jesus told the friends. "I'm going to choose some special helpers." He chose a man named Peter and his brother, Andrew. He chose two more men who were brothers, James and John. Jesus asked other men to be His special helpers, too—until there were twelve.

After that, Jesus always took His special helpers with Him to help Him pray for all the people who needed help.

Jesus was glad that He had talked with God about the men He chose to help Him.

Thank You, Jesus, for always helping me when I have to choose. I don't know how to pick but You do. Amen.

"Fill the Jars with Water."

Jesus told the servants, "Fill the jars with water."
When the jars had been filled to the brim, he said,
"Dip some out and take it to the master of ceremonies."

John 2:7–8 NLT

One day, Jesus' mother was a guest at a wedding celebration in a village called Cana. Jesus and His followers were there, too. But the wine ran out before the feast was over. Jesus' mother told Him, "They have no more wine." And she said to the servants, "Do whatever he tells you."

Six stone water pots were there. They were used for Jewish religious ceremonies and held twenty to thirty gallons each. Jesus told the servants, "Fill the jars with water." They filled the jars to the brim.

Then Jesus said, "Dip some out and take it to the man in charge of the feast." The man tasted what he thought was water, but Jesus had turned it to wine!

This was the first miracle Jesus ever did. Why do you think Jesus did this miracle? It was a sign showing who Jesus is. Jesus did miracles like these to show His glory and power and to help people believe in Him.

Dear God,
thank You for miracles that show me Your power.

"...Unless You Are Born Again."

Jesus replied, "I assure you, unless you are born again,
you can never see the Kingdom of God."
"What do you mean?" exclaimed Nicodemus.

JOHN 3:3–4 NLT

When you have a question, don't you think your teacher should have the answer? Nicodemus was a teacher for all of Israel. But when Jesus said, "You have to be born again," Nicodemus didn't know what this meant. Jesus told him that it is difficult to explain. It is like trying to follow the wind. We can hear and feel the wind, but we don't know where it came from or where it is going.

By believing in Jesus, a person has a second birth. This is sometimes called the new birth. When it happens, that person is born again. To see this new birth in a person's life, you must look carefully. It's like the wind—very hard to see.

Have you ever seen fruit hanging from a tree? Sometimes it is hard to see because the leaves hide it. A person who is born again has special fruit in his or her life. Look carefully and you may see love, joy, peace, patience, kindness, goodness, faithfulness, gentleness, and self-control. That is how you know if a person has been born again.

Dear God,

I want to please You— help me to grow all of Your good fruit in my life.

"Please Give Me a Drink."

Jesus, tired from the long walk, sat wearily beside the well about noontime. Soon a Samaritan woman came to draw water, and Jesus said to her, "Please give me a drink."

JOHN 4:6–7 NLT

It was about noon one day, and Jesus was alone, resting by a well. A woman came to the well to draw out some water. Jesus asked her to give Him some. In those days, this wasn't done. Men and women had nothing to do with each other unless they were married. Plus, the woman in this story was a Samaritan. Jesus was a Jew. The Jews thought they were much better than the Samaritans, and so they never spoke to each other.

Most women in those days got their water in the morning. Then they had what they needed for that day. Plus, they didn't have to carry water in the heat of the day. But this woman was an outcast in her village. She had been married several times. The other women stayed away from her because she was a sinner.

You might say this woman had three strikes against her. She was a sinner. She was a Samaritan. She was a woman. To everyone else, she was out, but not to Jesus. This story shows that Jesus came for the outcasts of this world. He came for sinners and poor people. He came for everyone, no matter who they are.

Dear God,
thank You for not
playing favorites—
You care for everyone.

The Big "If"

"If you forgive others for the things they do wrong,
then your Father in heaven will also forgive
you for the things you do wrong."

MATTHEW 6:14 ICB

Has someone ever made you really mad? You knew you should forgive that person, but you just didn't want to! You wanted to stay mad! Why should you forgive, after the mean thing he did?

Forgiving people is the right thing to do, and it makes God happy. But there are two other reasons you should forgive.

The first reason is in our verse. It says *if* you forgive others, then God will forgive you, too. "If" means it's a choice. You don't have to do it. But if you do, then God will forgive you for your sins. That means if you don't forgive, God won't either. That's probably part of the reason it makes God sad when we don't forgive. He loves to forgive us.

The second reason is that forgiving makes *us* feel better. It doesn't make the wrong thing that person did okay. But when we stay mad, it makes our tummies hurt and we become not-so-nice people. Then we might go around making others mad, too, just as the person who hurt you did!

So forgive others, then God can forgive you. We all make mistakes and need forgiveness.

Dear God,

help me to not stay mad at people, but help me forgive them. Thank You for forgiving me when I forgive others.

No Worries

"So don't worry. Don't say, 'What will we eat?'
Or, 'What will we drink?' Or, 'What will we wear?'
People who are ungodly run after all of those things.
Your Father who is in heaven knows that you need them."

Matthew 6:31–32 NIrV

What things worry you? Maybe being left with a new babysitter? Or a hard test at school? Or listening to your parents argue? There are plenty of things that cause us to worry. So what can you do when worry takes over?

When you feel that yucky worry feeling sneaking up on you, the best thing you can do is pray. If something bothers you, then it matters to God, too. He cares about whatever makes His children feel bad. But He's not at all surprised by our worries! Our verse says that God knows exactly what we need and what worries us, and He will take good care of us. So we don't need to worry like people who don't know God. They don't understand how powerful God is and how much He can help them. But we know we can trust God to fill all our needs. No worries!

So next time worry creeps into your mind, remember to turn to God. Ask Him to help you not be afraid. He loves to take care of you, and you can trust Him to make your worries disappear. What a relief!

God,

I know I can trust You, but sometimes I still worry. Help me to talk to You about my worries and help me not to be afraid.

"Just Ask Believing"

"Just say the word, and my servant will be healed."

MATTHEW 8:8 NIV

When we pray, we need to believe that God will answer our prayer. A soldier in the army believed that Jesus could answer a prayer. The soldier knew Jesus needed only to speak and his prayer would be answered.

Jesus was walking into the city of Capernaum. An important soldier ran to meet Him. "Jesus," the soldier said, "my helper is very sick. He cannot move and is in much pain." The soldier was worried because he was afraid his helper would die.

"I will come to your house and make your helper well," Jesus said.

"No, Jesus. I can see how busy You are," the soldier said. "You do not need to come all the way to my house. If You will just say that my helper is well, I know that he will be healed."

Jesus was surprised. He turned to the people who were with Him. "This man believes in Me more than anyone," He said.

Then Jesus turned to the soldier. "Go home," He said. "Because you believe in Me, your helper is already over his sickness."

When the soldier returned home, he found his helper completely well. The soldier had believed that Jesus could answer his prayer.

Dear Jesus,

help me believe that You can answer my prayers— even when I cannot see You answering them. Thank You for caring for me and loving me. Amen.

"Lord, Save Us!"

The disciples went and woke him, saying,
"Lord, save us! We're going to drown!"
MATTHEW 8:25 NIV

When we are afraid, we can pray. One time, Jesus' disciples prayed when they were caught in a bad storm.

Jesus had been teaching people about God. He was very tired from His busy day.

He and His disciples climbed into a small fishing boat and sailed onto the lake. Jesus was so tired that He went to the back of the boat and laid down for a nap.

Suddenly, a storm came up. The wind began to blow. The waves rocked the boat. The wind and the waves made it hard for the disciples to stand up. The boat was beginning to fill with water.

Even though some of the disciples were big, strong fishermen, they were afraid. They woke Jesus and said, "Lord, save us! We are going to drown!"

"Why are you afraid?" Jesus asked. "Don't you know I will always take care of you—no matter how bad the storm gets?"

Jesus stood up and stretched out His arms. He told the wind to stop blowing. He told the waves to be still and stop rocking the boat. Suddenly, everything was quiet.

The disciples were surprised that Jesus could make the storm obey Him. They were no longer afraid.

Dear God,

thank You for always being nearby, watching over me. When I'm afraid, help me to remember that You are taking care of me. Amen.

"Have Mercy on Us"

As Jesus went on from there, two blind men followed him,
calling out, "Have mercy on us, Son of David!"

Matthew 9:27 niv

Jesus wants us to pray about everything—big things and small things. Two blind men believed that Jesus could make them see again, and Jesus heard their prayer.

Everywhere in the town, people were talking about Jesus and His miracles. Crowds of people started following Him around, trying to hear what He had to say.

At the end of the day, Jesus was tired and wanted to rest. Step, step, step went Jesus' sandals as He walked toward the house where He would spend the night.

Swish, swish, swish! Two blind men slowly moved along behind Him. They called out to Jesus, "Have mercy on us, Son of David!"

Jesus went into the house and the two blind men followed. When Jesus turned around, He saw the blind men. "Do you believe that I can do this?" He asked them.

"Yes, Lord, we believe," they said.

Jesus touched their eyes and said, "If you believe, it will happen to you."

Suddenly, the blind men could see. Jesus had heard their prayer. Jesus told them not to tell anyone what happened. But they were too happy for that. They told everyone they met that Jesus had touched their eyes—and now they could see.

Jesus,

I believe in You! I know that You can do anything— big things and small things. Help me remember to pray when I need Your help.

Amen.

Loaves and Fish

[Jesus] took the five loaves and the two fish and,
looking to heaven, he thanked God for the food.

MATTHEW 14:19 NCV

God wants us to thank Him for the food we eat—just like Jesus did. Jesus and His disciples sat down to rest on a hillside one day. Before they knew it, a lot of people had gathered around. They wanted Jesus to tell them about God.

Jesus started to teach them. Soon, many people were sitting on the grassy hill, listening to Him. They listened until suppertime. They didn't even notice they were hungry until Jesus stopped talking.

"We should send these people home so they can eat supper," Jesus' disciples said to Him.

But Jesus said to His disciples, "They are too far from home. We must give them something to eat."

"What?" the disciples said. "We don't have any food!"

Just then Andrew said, "This little boy says he wants to share his supper. But it is only five little loaves of bread and two fish. It is enough to feed only a few."

Jesus took the little boy's supper and thanked God for the food. Then He began to break the bread and fish into pieces. Soon there were hundreds and hundreds of pieces of bread and fish—enough to feed all the hungry people.

Heavenly Father,

thank You for giving me food to eat. Help me to share my food with those who are hungry. Amen.

"People Need More Than Bread."

Then the Devil came and said to him, "If you are the Son of God, change these stones into loaves of bread." But Jesus told him, "No! The Scriptures say, 'People need more than bread for their life; they must feed on every word of God.'"

MATTHEW 4:3–4 NLT

TWO things we cannot live without are food and water. Even Jesus got hungry. But He knew that people needed two kinds of food. There is food for the body and food for the soul. Everyone knows about the food for our body. Jesus came to teach us about the other food. In fact, it was one of the first things He talked about. "People need more than bread for their life," Jesus said. "They must feed on every word of God."

One day Jesus was out in the countryside. Thousands of people came there to see and hear Him. When it came time to eat, no one had any food. With five loaves of bread and two fish, Jesus fed them all. The same people crowded around Jesus the next day. He told them, "You only came here because I fed you yesterday. But God gives you the true bread from heaven."

"Please, give us this bread," they begged.

Jesus answered them, "I am the bread of life. Come to me and you will never be hungry."

No one can go without food. No one should go without knowing that Jesus is the real food.

Dear God,

help me to remember that Jesus is the real Bread of Life.

Big Brother

"Anyone who does what my Father in heaven
wants is my brother or sister or mother."
Matthew 12:50 NIrV

How many people are in your family?

Did you know you have a brother that you might not have counted?

Once, when Jesus was talking to some people, He told them that anyone who obeys God is part of His family. Do you obey God? Then you're Jesus' brother or sister! It's fun to be part of God's family. God is our Father in heaven and Jesus is His Son. Since we're God's children, too, that makes Jesus our Big Brother.

Some big brothers are pests. Jesus isn't that kind of brother. He's the kind who sticks up for you when other kids tease you. He'll listen to you if something's bothering you. He laughs and plays with you. He does all these things, only you can't see Him! But He's not make-believe at all. He's real!

Jesus loves children. He especially loves those who do what His Father says in His Word. Someday He'll come back for you so you can live forever with Him in His house. So keep obeying God and enjoy having such an awesome Big Brother.

Jesus,

thank You for being the best Big Brother ever. Help me to obey God so I can be ready to live with You when You come back for me.

"She Is Only Sleeping"

[Jairus] begged Jesus, "Please come. My little daughter is dying. Place your hands on her to heal her. Then she will live."

MARK 5:23 NIrv

Jesus wants us to pray and tell Him about our sick friends and family. Jesus listened to Jairus and made his daughter well—even when people didn't think He could.

Splish, splash went the water as Jesus stepped off the boat and onto the shore. When Jairus saw Jesus, he came running to Him and bowed down.

"My little daughter is very sick," Jairus told Jesus. "Please come and put Your hands on her. Then she will be made well."

On the way to Jairus's house, a man came running toward them. "Don't bother Jesus," he said to Jairus. "Your little girl died."

Jesus kept walking. "Don't be afraid," he told Jairus. "Trust Me. She is only sleeping."

When Jesus reached Jairus's house, He saw the little girl lying on the bed. Her eyes were closed. She was very still.

Jesus took her by the hand and said, "Little girl, listen to Me. Get up!"

All of a sudden, the little girl's eyes opened. She stood up and walked around.

Jesus turned to the girl's mother and said, "I think she's hungry. Give her something to eat."

Jesus knew He could make Jairus's daughter well—and He did!

Thank You, Jesus, for keeping me well. When my friends or family members are sick, help me remember to tell You about them. You can make them well. Amen.

A Silent Prayer

She thought, "I just need to touch his clothes.
Then I will be healed."
MARK 5:28 NIrV

Sometimes we pray aloud, and sometimes we think a prayer. Jesus hears every prayer—the ones we think and the ones we say out loud. Jesus heard a prayer from a woman that no one else heard.

Everywhere Jesus went, a crowd of people followed Him. Some wanted Jesus to make them well, and some wanted Jesus to tell them more about God.

In the crowd one day was a woman who had been sick for twelve years. She had been to many doctors, but they could not make her well. She was not getting better. She heard about Jesus and wanted to see if He could help her.

"I just need to touch His clothes," she thought. "Then I will be healed."

Suddenly, the woman reached out and touched Jesus' clothes. Something wonderful happened! The sickness left her.

No one had heard her prayer. No one—but Jesus! He turned and looked into the crowd. "Who touched Me?" He asked.

Then the woman came and fell at His feet. She was shaking with fear, but she told Jesus what she had done.

Jesus said to her, "Dear woman, you believed in Me and you are made well."

Dear Jesus,

thank You for hearing my prayers—whether I think them or say them out loud. Help me remember that You can do all things. Amen.

"I Do Believe!"

Immediately the father cried out, "I do believe!
Help me to believe more!"

MARK 9:24 NCV

God wants us to believe with all our hearts that He will answer our prayers. He waited for one worried dad to say the words before He healed his son.

There was a big crowd of people around Jesus. They wanted to hear what He had to say. In the crowd was a man with a sick boy, who wanted to talk to Jesus.

"I brought my son to You," he said to Jesus. "He cannot hear or speak. I asked Your special helpers to make him well, but they could not."

"How long has your boy had this sickness?" asked Jesus.

"Since he was a young child," answered the father. "I love him so much. If You can do anything, show us kindness. Please help us."

"Do you believe that I can make your boy well?" Jesus asked. "Anything is possible if you believe."

Tears came to the father's eyes. Right away he said, "I do believe! Help me to believe more!"

Then Jesus looked at the boy. "Sickness, come out and never go back in again!" He commanded.

The boy was completely healed when his dad said the words "I believe!"

Thank You,

Jesus, for answering my prayers. Help me believe in You with all my heart. Amen.

"Have Mercy on Me!"

[Bartimaeus] began to shout, "Jesus, Son of David, have mercy on me!"

MARK 10:47 NIV

Sometimes we pray for a big miracle. Sometimes we pray for a small miracle. Bartimaeus received a big miracle from Jesus.

Bartimaeus sat by the roadside. He felt the soft grass, but he could not see it. He heard the birds singing, but he could not see them.

One day, Bartimaeus heard people shouting, "Jesus is coming!" He heard the *swish, swish* of Jesus' sandals, but he could not see Him. Bartimaeus was blind.

He began to shout, "Jesus, Jesus!"

The people standing nearby said, "Be quiet."

But Bartimaeus shouted louder, "Jesus, have mercy on me!"

Jesus stopped. He told the people to bring the blind man to Him. The people called to Bartimaeus, "Get up! Jesus is calling you."

Bartimaeus threw off his coat and jumped to his feet. He moved toward Jesus.

Jesus looked at the blind man and asked, "What do you want Me to do?"

"Please help me see," answered Bartimaeus.

Jesus said to him, "Go. You are able to see now."

Bartimaeus's eyes were opened. He saw the blue sky above and the birds sitting in the branches of the trees. He saw the people. "I can see! I can see!" he shouted as he followed Jesus down the road.

Dear God,

thank You for giving me eyes to see the beautiful world You have made. Help me to be thankful for miracles—big ones and small ones. Amen.

"...Everything She Has."

Then a poor widow came and dropped in two pennies. [Jesus] called his disciples to him and said, "I assure you, this poor widow has given more than all the others have given. For they gave a tiny part of their surplus, but she, poor as she is, has given everything she has."

MARK 12:42–44 NLT

In the ancient temple, money was collected to give to the poor. This poor widow who gave all her money at the temple is like another widow in the Bible.

The prophet Elijah went to a town called Zarephath. There he saw a widow gathering sticks. He asked her, "Would you bring me a cup of water and a bite of bread?"

"I'll tell you the truth," she answered. "I have no bread in my house. I do have a handful of flour left in the jar and a little cooking oil in the bottom of the jug. I was gathering a few sticks to cook my last meal. Then my son and I will die."

Elijah told her, "Don't be afraid. Cook your meal, but first bake a loaf of bread for me. There will be enough food for you. The Lord tells me you will have flour and oil left over."

The widow did this, and she, Elijah, and her son ate for many days. No matter how much flour and oil they used, there was always enough left over.

These two widows teach us to not be afraid to give to others. When we do, God will take care of everything we need.

Dear God,

help me to give to others as the widow and her son did.

Ask Jesus to Help

[Peter's] mother-in-law was suffering from a high fever,
and they asked Jesus to help her.

LUKE 4:38 NIV

When we pray for the sick, Jesus will help them. Simon Peter asked for help when his wife's mother got sick with a fever.

Jesus had been teaching the people about God, His Father, all day long. When He finished, He looked around. "Where is Simon Peter?" Jesus asked the other disciples.

Swish, swish went Jesus' sandals as He walked to Peter's house. When He got there, He found Peter waiting.

"Please, Jesus, pray for my wife's mother. She is so sick. Can You make her well again?" Simon asked.

Jesus stood by the woman's bed. He looked down at her and prayed for her. Suddenly, her fever went away. She got out of bed and said she had work to do in the kitchen. Everyone was surprised.

When the neighbors heard what Jesus had done, they brought all the sick people in their families to Jesus. He gently touched each one. Just like that, they were well again.

Finally, Jesus went away to rest. He was very tired. But other people came with their sick loved ones. They searched for Jesus until they found Him.

Dear Jesus,

help me remember to pray for people who are sick. I know You can make them well again. Thank You for making me well when I am sick. Amen.

"Seeing Their Faith. . ."

So they went up to the roof, took off some tiles, and lowered
the sick man down into the crowd, still on his mat, right in
front of Jesus. Seeing their faith, Jesus said to the man,
"Son, your sins are forgiven."

<small>LUKE 5:19–20 TLB</small>

One day while Jesus was teaching, some religious leaders were sitting nearby. Such men were always around. They came from every village and from as far away as Jerusalem. Some other men came to where Jesus was teaching, carrying a paralyzed man on a mat. They couldn't push through the crowd to Jesus, so they went up to the roof and opened a hole. They lowered the sick man down into the crowd right in front of Jesus. Jesus said to the man, "Son, your sins are forgiven."

The religious leaders said to each other, "Who does this man think He is? He is mocking God! Only God can forgive sins."

Jesus knew what they were thinking. He asked them, "Is it easier to say, 'Your sins are forgiven' or 'Get up and walk'? I'll prove that I have the power to forgive sins."

Then Jesus said to the paralyzed man, "Stand up. Take your mat, and go on home. You're healed!" Everyone watched as the man jumped up and went home praising God.

Jesus healed many people in His day. But this was not the reason He came. This story plainly shows why God sent Jesus to us. It was to take care of the problem of sin.

Dear God,
thank You for sending Your son, Jesus, to forgive our sins.

The Best Reward

"So love your enemies. Do good to them, and lend to them without hoping to get anything back. If you do these things, you will have a great reward."

LUKE 6:35 ICB

Have you ever seen a poster offering a reward for a lost dog? If the reward is ten dollars, you might keep your eyes open for the puppy. But if it were a thousand dollars, you might spend *lots* of extra time trying to find it! The amount of the reward tells you how important something is to the person offering it. The bigger the reward, the more important your help is to that person.

The Bible tells how we can earn a huge reward. All we have to do is love our enemies and do good to them. If we lend them something, we shouldn't worry if they don't give it back. If we do these things, we'll have a great reward. Who do you think put up that reward poster? God posted it in our Bibles in Luke 6:35. And since He offers such a huge reward, we know it's important to Him that we do it.

Is it easy to love your enemies? No. Finding a lost dog isn't easy either. But doing what God asks is always worth the reward He offers—living forever with Him! That's better than a million dollars!

God,

it's hard to love people
I don't like. Help me to love
them anyway and to look
for something good in them.
I want Your reward.

"Anyone Who Listens. . ."

"Anyone who listens to my teaching and obeys me is wise,
like a person who builds a house on solid rock."

MATTHEW 7:24 NLT

Jesus taught there are two kinds of food. The food for our body is very important. It should be healthy food because it builds our bodies. If we use bad food, our bodies will be unhealthy. Foods with too much sugar and fat can't build a healthy body. There is also food for our soul. The best food for our soul is Jesus. When we believe in Jesus, He is food to our soul and makes our spirits strong.

We also have two kinds of houses. The houses or apartments we live in give shelter to our bodies. If they aren't built well, we could get cold, wet, or sick. There is also a spiritual house, which no one sees. This house is built upon what we hear and what we do.

By reading the Bible, we hear the words of Jesus. For example, He said, "Do for others what you would like them to do for you." You can build your life on these words. Jesus said that these words explain all that is taught in the Bible. This is the Golden Rule. If you hear this rule and do it, your spiritual house won't fall.

Dear God,
I want to make my spiritual house strong—help me to follow the Golden Rule.

Kingdom Kid

"So don't be afraid, little flock. For it gives your
Father great happiness to give you the Kingdom."
LUKE 12:32 NLT

Some days it seems as if nothing goes right. You get in trouble for things that you didn't mean to do. It might even seem as if God is trying to trick you and make you mess up. Guess what? God is on your side. He wants to help you do the right thing. He wants you to be in His kingdom, and He can't wait to spend forever with you.

Our verse says it makes God really happy to give His kingdom to you. He looks forward to the day when He'll send Jesus back to the earth to set up this kingdom. It's going to be a huge party, and you'll be one of His kingdom kids! You'll be a prince or princess! We'll enjoy a wonderful meal together with believers from all over the world. We'll even get to see people who loved Jesus but died before He returned. They'll be alive again, and it will be a wonderful celebration.

Most of all, we'll get to live with God. Just like us, He looks forward to that great day when we can live together forever. What a happy day that will be!

God,

I'm glad You want to be with me forever. That's what I want, too. I have a big hug to give You when I see You in Your kingdom.

"And Suddenly All Was Calm."

And Jesus answered, "Why are you afraid?
You have so little faith!" Then he stood up and rebuked
the wind and waves, and suddenly all was calm.

MATTHEW 8:26 NLT

Do you know how to swim? Some of Jesus' followers didn't. One time when they were in a boat on a big lake, the wind began to tip the boat. It was filling with water! They were afraid even though Jesus was in the same boat. He wasn't afraid of the storm. In fact, He was asleep! His followers were afraid because they believed more in the storm than in Jesus. So Jesus scolded them, "You have so little faith!" They believed in the wrong thing.

Many people today believe in the wrong thing. They have little faith in Jesus and great faith in the world. Hard times can come to us in this world. They are like the storm in this story. Jesus may seem to be sleeping through your storm, but you should always believe in Him. Maybe the storm has come to help you believe in Him even more.

Jesus' followers cried out, "Lord, save us!" They did just the right thing. The Bible says, "Anyone who calls on the name of the Lord will be saved."

Dear God,

thank You for saving us
when we have faith in You.

"They Were Like Sheep."

And wherever he went, he healed people of every sort of disease
and illness. He felt great pity for the crowds that came. . . .
They were like sheep without a shepherd.

MATTHEW 9:35–36 NLT

Jesus was born in Israel because He was a Jew. He loves all people, but He first came to His own people—the Jews. To God, they are like a flock of sheep. Jesus came to be their shepherd and bring them back to God. The leaders of Israel at the time only took care of themselves. God's sheep had no shepherd.

Long before Jesus came, a man named Ezekiel asked them:

"Shouldn't you shepherds take care of God's people? You have all you need, but you don't take care of the flock. You haven't strengthened the weak, healed the sick, or bandaged the injured. You haven't brought back the stray sheep or searched for the lost. You've ruled Israel harshly and brutally. They were scattered because there was no shepherd. Then they became food for wild animals. My sheep wandered all over the mountains and on every hill. They were scattered over the whole earth, and no one searched or looked for them."

This is why Jesus came. He said, "I have come to seek and save those who are lost." He is the Good Shepherd who loves all people.

Dear God,
thank You for being the Good Shepherd.

"...Produce a Huge Harvest."

"The good soil represents the hearts of those who truly accept God's message and produce a huge harvest—thirty, sixty, or even a hundred times as much as had been planted."

MATTHEW 13:23 NLT

Jesus talked about ordinary things to teach people about God. He didn't try to confuse anyone. He wanted the invisible, spiritual things to be clear so that we could understand them. He also gave ordinary acts spiritual meaning so that our lives could remind us of God.

The parable of the sower is about a farmer planting seed. But this was not a vegetable garden, where seeds are planted one by one. This farmer was in a big field planting wheat. He carried a bag of seed over his shoulder. He dipped his big hand into the seed and tossed the seed onto the land. The seed landed on hard earth, in stony ground, in the weeds, or in good earth.

Later, Jesus explained this story. He said that the ground is your heart and the seed is God's Word. Some hearts are hard. The truth of God can't even start growing there. Hearts with no room for Jesus are like ground filled with stones or weeds.

So you might wonder about your heart. Can the seed of the Word grow there? Simply pray every day that God will soften your heart. Ask the Lord to remove the stones and weeds. The Lord will do this, and then the Word of God can grow in you!

Dear God,

please soften my heart and let Your Word grow in me!

"...Walking on the Water."

About three o'clock in the morning Jesus came to them,
walking on the water.

MATTHEW 14:25 NLT

Jesus' followers were once taught a lesson on how to trust the Lord.

One day, Jesus was alone on a mountain praying. Some of His followers were in a boat, rowing across a huge lake. Nighttime came, and the boat was far away from land. They were having trouble rowing because of strong winds. Jesus came to help them late at night. He was walking on the water! The disciples saw Him and screamed. They thought Jesus was a ghost.

Jesus said, "It's all right. I'm here! Don't be afraid."

Peter, one of the men in the boat, called out, "Lord, if it's You, tell me to come to You by walking on water."

"Come on," Jesus said.

Peter went over the side of the boat and walked on the water toward Jesus! But then he looked around at the high waves and was terrified. As soon as Peter took his eyes off Jesus, he began to sink. He shouted, "Save me, Lord!"

Jesus reached out and grabbed Peter. "You don't have much faith," Jesus said. "Why did you doubt me?" They climbed back into the boat, and the wind stopped.

Peter lost faith for a simple reason. Instead of looking at Jesus, he looked at the waves. We must never stop looking to Jesus, or we might sink, too!

Dear God,
help me to keep
my eyes on You
and Your son,
Jesus Christ.

"His Face Shone Like the Sun."

As the men watched, Jesus' appearance changed so that his face
shone like the sun, and his clothing became dazzling white.

MATTHEW 17:2 NLT

Jesus Christ was God who came to live with us as a man. He looked like an ordinary man. Everyone knew He came from a town called Nazareth. This was just an ordinary place. He was raised in a carpenter's home with brothers and sisters. Nearly no one knew that Jesus was God.

One day, Jesus went with three of His followers to the top of a mountain. There, Peter, James, and John saw something that no one had seen before. They saw Jesus as God. His face shone like the sun, and His body was white light.

Just then, two other men appeared with Jesus. Both of them had lived hundreds of years before. One was Moses, the great leader of Israel. The other was Elijah, the prophet. Peter wanted to set up tents to worship Moses, Elijah, and Jesus. But God put a stop to this saying, "This is my beloved Son, and I am fully pleased with him. Listen to him."

This happened so people would know that the old way was past. There was no reason to worship anyone other than Jesus. Moses and Elijah had done their jobs. Now Jesus would finish God's plan.

Dear God,
help me to remember that You alone should be worshipped.

"You're Welcome!"

"Anyone who welcomes a little child
like this in my name welcomes me."

MATTHEW 18:5 NIrV

Do you know that children are some of Jesus' favorite people? He loves them so much He told grown-ups they need to become like them if they want to get into the kingdom of heaven!

One day, Jesus' helpers asked Him, "Who is the most important person in the kingdom of heaven?" (Matthew 18:1 NIrV). Jesus called a little child to come and stand by Him. He probably knelt down, put His arm around the child, and snuggled him close. He told His helpers to listen up because what He was about to tell them was the truth. He said, "You need to change and become like little children. If you don't, you will never enter the kingdom of heaven. Anyone who becomes as free of pride as this child is the most important in the kingdom of heaven" (Matthew 18:3–4 NIrV).

Then He added with a smile, "Anyone who welcomes a little child like this in my name welcomes me" (Matthew 18:5 NIrV).

To welcome someone means you're glad they came. Children were important to Jesus in Bible times. And you're important to Him today! He'll welcome you into His arms and His kingdom when you let Him be in charge of your life.

God,

I want to be in Your kingdom. Help me to let You be in charge of my life. I love You.

"Now He Is Found."

"We must celebrate with a feast, for this son of mine was dead
and has now returned to life. He was lost, but now he is found."

LUKE 15:23–24 NLT

A man had two sons. The younger one told his father, "I want my share of your money now, instead of waiting until you die." So the father divided his wealth between his sons.

A few days later, the younger son packed up and took a long vacation. He wasted all of his money and lived a wild life. Then his money ran out, and he began to starve. He got a job feeding pigs, but he was so hungry that even the pigs' food looked good to him.

The son finally came to his senses. "At home, even the servants have food to eat," he said. So he went home to his father.

The father saw his son coming from far away. He was filled with love for his son, and he ran to him and hugged and kissed him. His son said, "Father, I've sinned against you. I shouldn't be called your son anymore." But his father put the finest clothes on him. He put a ring on his finger and sandals on his feet. The whole household celebrated with a feast. "My son was dead and has returned to life," he said with joy. "He was lost. But now he is found."

Jesus told this story to show how much God loves us.

Dear God,

thank You for Your love and forgiveness.

"...a Man There Named Zacchaeus."

There was a man there named Zacchaeus. . . . He tried to get a look at Jesus, but he was too short to see over the crowds. So he ran ahead and climbed a sycamore tree beside the road.

LUKE 19:2–4 NLT

In our country, many people love celebrities like movie stars and rock stars. These famous people are usually good looking. They are often tall and well dressed. You don't see very many short or ugly celebrities. But God doesn't care what anyone looks like. What matters most to God is your heart. He wants you to love Him and seek Him, just like Zacchaeus did.

Here's how Zacchaeus met the Lord. Jesus was traveling to Jerusalem for the last time. He passed through Jericho, where Zacchaeus lived. Zacchaeus was an important tax collector in town, so he was very rich. He wanted to see Jesus as He passed by. But Zacchaeus was too short to see over the crowds. So he ran ahead and climbed a sycamore tree beside the road. He could watch from there.

Zacchaeus probably looked silly in that tree. He was a grown man and a rich man, too. But he didn't care what people thought of him. He just wanted to see Jesus. When Jesus came by, He saw Zacchaeus in the tree and called him by name. "Zacchaeus!" He said. "Quick, come down! I want to stay in your home today."

Of all the people crowding the street that day, Jesus saw Zacchaeus. Why? Because Zacchaeus so badly wanted to see the Lord.

Dear God,

I want to be like Zacchaeus—help me always to look for You!

"Hosanna in the Highest!"

"Hosanna to the Son of David!" "Blessed is he who comes in
the name of the Lord!" "Hosanna in the highest!"

MATTHEW 21:9 NIV

Praising God is part of praying. The people sang praises to Jesus as He came into the city of Jerusalem.

Step, step, step! Jesus and His special helpers were going to the temple. On the way, Jesus stopped and said, "There is a little donkey in the city. Untie it and bring it to Me."

Jesus' helpers did just as He asked them. They found the donkey and brought it back to Jesus. Jesus climbed on the donkey's back and rode it into the city.

Clippety-clop, clippety-clop went the donkey's feet. Jesus' helpers walked along the road beside Him.

Many other people were walking along the road. They were happy to see Jesus!

Some people spread their coats on the road. Other people cut branches from palm trees and laid them on the road. This showed that they believed that Jesus was a real, true king.

Some other people ran ahead to the city. "Jesus is coming! Jesus is coming!" they shouted. When they heard the shouts, still more people came to see Jesus. They sang praises to Him, "Hosanna! Hosanna in the highest!"

What a happy day it was! Everyone who loved Jesus praised Him by singing happy songs.

Thank You, God, for sending Your Son, Jesus. Help me to be happy and show my love to Jesus by singing praises. Help me tell others about Jesus' love. Amen.

". . .on Ahead to Pray."

Then Jesus brought them to an olive grove called Gethsemane,
and he said, "Sit here while I go on ahead to pray."

MATTHEW 26:36 NLT

Jesus often took His followers to rest and pray in the Garden of Gethsemane. They were there praying on the night before Jesus died. The days before this night had made Jesus very tired. But the next day would be the hardest day of His life—the day He died. He was so weary that an angel came from heaven to help Him.

You may have heard people talk of angels or seen pictures of angels. They don't often show up in Bible stories. Angels appear only when something very important is happening in God's plan. The most important thing that ever happened was Jesus' life. Angels were there right from the beginning. An angel told both Mary and Joseph about Jesus' birth.

Jesus once spent forty days alone in the wilderness. There, He didn't eat, but He prayed. When this time was over, angels came to help Him. The next time angels appeared was here in Gethsemane. Angels were there when Jesus came back to life, too. There was an earthquake when an angel came to Jesus' grave. The Bible says this angel looked like lightning and his clothes were white as snow.

We shouldn't expect angels to appear again until Jesus comes back. Then, Jesus said, "I will come in the glory of my Father with his angels."

Dear God,

help me to focus only on You and Your son— and nothing else.

"...with Me in Paradise."

Then he said, "Jesus, remember me when you come into
your Kingdom." And Jesus replied, "I assure you,
today you will be with me in paradise."

LUKE 23:42–43 NLT

It is never too late to believe in Jesus. When Jesus died, two criminals were crucified with Him. Each one hung on a cross. One was on Jesus' right side, the other on His left.

One of the criminals made fun of the Lord. "So you're the Messiah, are you?" he sneered. "Prove it! Save yourself, and save us, too."

But the other criminal didn't like this. "You're dying," he said to the mocking criminal. "Don't you fear God even now? We did evil things and deserve to die. But this man hasn't done anything wrong." Then he said, "Jesus, remember me when you come into your Kingdom." Jesus replied, "I promise you, today you will be with me in paradise."

The criminal died that day. The last thing he did was to believe in Jesus, and now he is in paradise with Him!

Dear God,
thank You for accepting anyone who believes on You, no matter when.

"Hear Our Prayer, O Lord"

They all came together regularly to pray.

ACTS 1:14 NIrV

We can pray with our family every day, and we can pray with others at church each week. After Jesus went to heaven, His special helpers found out how important it was to pray together.

Jesus' special helpers didn't know what to do without Jesus. It seemed like they were all alone. They felt lonely and afraid.

One day, the helpers went upstairs to the room where they were staying. They remembered that Jesus had told them how important it was to pray and talk to God. So the helpers decided that every day, they would pray right there in that room, for themselves and for others.

Soon some women came to pray with them. Jesus' mother, Mary, and His brothers came, too. Other people who believed in Jesus heard and came to the upstairs room to pray.

The people prayed for the sick and those who needed help. They prayed for God to keep them safe. They prayed for those who wanted to hurt them. By praying, they learned what God wanted them to do and how they could tell others about Jesus.

Every day more people came to pray. They learned that when they prayed together they no longer felt lonely or afraid.

Dear God,

thank You that I can pray with my family every day. Thank You for my church where I can go and pray with my friends. Amen.

"Who Are You, Lord?"

"Who are you, Lord?" Saul asked.

Acts 9:5 niv

There was an important man in town named Saul. He said that he loved and respected God. But he did not think that Jesus was God's Son. Saul was angry that so many people were following Jesus! He did his best to keep them from telling others about Jesus.

"I will go to other cities and stop people from talking about Jesus," Saul said. "I will put them in jail if I have to!" Saul and his friends got on their horses and headed for a city called Damascus.

On the road, Saul and his friends saw a very bright light. Saul was shocked and surprised! He fell to the ground. The light was so bright that Saul could not see anything!

Then Saul heard a voice. "Saul, why are you hurting Me?"

"Who are You?" asked Saul.

The voice said, "I am Jesus, the one you are hurting."

Then Saul's friends took him to the house of a man who loved Jesus. For three days, Saul stayed there and prayed.

God sent a man to find Saul and pray for him. Suddenly, Saul could see again! He was so sorry that he had hurt those who loved Jesus. He began telling people that Jesus was God's Son.

Dear Jesus,

I love You. Thank You for loving me. Help me to obey You and to tell other people that You love them, too.

Amen.

Good from Bad

We know that in everything God works for the good of those who love him. They are the people God called, because that was his plan.

ROMANS 8:28 ICB

Sometimes really bad things happen to people, even very nice people who love God. It's hard to understand. There aren't any answers to why those things happen. They just do. Parents lose jobs, people get sick and die, bad storms come, and some moms and dads get divorced. Those are scary times in our lives.

But there's always hope, if you love God. He can do anything! He can even make good things come from bad situations. Our verse today promises that in *everything* "God works for the good of those who love him." Everything! Even if it's a bad thing, God can turn it around and make something good come from it. Things may not end up as they were before, but there will be a new kind of good for you, perhaps even better than it was before. Maybe you'll learn something that will help you in your life, or maybe you'll become better friends with God because of it.

So when things are going rough and bad things happen, remember you can trust God to work things out for your good. Because you love Him, and He loves you.

God, when things change, sometimes I get scared. I want things to stay the same. Help me to trust You to bring good out of what seems bad.

Yes-Man

Thank You, Jesus, for dying on the cross for my sins.

God has made a great many promises.
They are all "Yes" because of what Christ has done.
2 CORINTHIANS 1:20 NIrV

Have you ever heard of a "yes-man"? It's someone who does whatever someone tells him to do. He agrees with whatever that person says. That can be dangerous because the person he agrees with may ask him to do something he shouldn't.

But we can always say yes to God. He is always right. He'll never ask us to do something wrong. Jesus was God's best yes-man. He never sinned, because He always did what His Father asked. Our Bible verse says God made many promises. Jesus stamped His "yes" on each promise because He believed whatever God said would happen. God asked Jesus to do many of the same things He asks us to do. He wanted Jesus to obey His parents, be kind to others, and be friends with Him. But then God asked Jesus to do something He will *never* ask us to do. He asked Jesus to die for our sins. Jesus trusted God so much He even said "yes" to that!

We can trust God, too. He loves us just as much as He loves Jesus. Will you be a yes-man for God?

God,

it's hard to trust Someone I can't see. Help me to say "yes" to whatever You ask me to do.

Under Construction

God began doing a good work in you.
And he will continue it until it is finished when
Jesus Christ comes again. I am sure of that.

PHILIPPIANS 1:6 ICB

Sometimes when workers fix a road, they put up a sign that says UNDER CONSTRUCTION. That means they're still working on the road, and it may be bumpy or dusty until it's done. We have to be patient until they're done working, and then the road will be better than ever.

You know what? God put an "Under Construction" sign on you! He started working on you when you were born. He's fixing all the things that aren't very nice about you. He's helping you be nicer by smoothing off the sharp pointed words you say that hurt people's feelings. He's carving your heart so you'll obey your parents the first time they ask you to do something. God's shaping you into the best boy or girl you can be.

When will God be done with you? Not until Jesus comes back. But you can be sure that He never gives up on you, even when you make mistakes. He just keeps patiently shaping you like a soft, giant piece of clay. So don't worry if you don't always do what you know you should. God isn't finished with you yet.

God, help me to be patient while You work on me. I want to be my very best for You. Thank You for not giving up on me.

Jesus in Me

The mystery in a nutshell is just this: Christ is in you, so therefore you can look forward to sharing in God's glory.

COLOSSIANS 1:27 MSG

Have you ever been told you look or act like your mom or dad? You might have your mom's hair color or your dad's funny laugh. That's because, when you were born, a little bit of them mixed together to become you! Kind of mysterious, huh?

The Bible talks about an even bigger mystery. Not only is a little bit of your mom and dad in you, but a little bit of Jesus is, too! When you love Jesus and ask Him to be in charge of your life, He comes to live inside your heart. Pretty soon you'll start looking and acting like Him. The nicest thing someone could ever say to you is, "You remind me of Jesus!"

When Jesus is in you, you can look forward to His coming back to rescue you from all the problems of this world. When He does, you'll become exactly like Him. That's what sharing in God's glory means. We won't sin anymore, we won't cry, we won't have bad thoughts. That day will be better than Christmas!

So keep loving Jesus and learning how He wants you to live. Pretty soon you'll be just like Him.

Thank You, God, for giving me something better than Christmas to look forward to. Help me to be more like Your Son, Jesus, every day.

Always Obey

Children, always obey your parents,
for this pleases the Lord.

COLOSSIANS 3:20 NLT

Has your mom or dad ever asked you not to do something, but you went ahead and did it anyway? Maybe you even pretended you didn't hear what your mom or dad said. How did you feel about that? Did it end up the way you wanted it to?

Usually, if you disobey a parent, you'll get in trouble. It's not a very happy ending for you or that parent. Why not obey even when you don't feel like it? You may feel a little angry at first, but later you'll notice a spark of happiness deep down inside. You'll know you did the right thing.

Our Bible verse says children must *always* obey their parents because this pleases the Lord. Doing what your parents say every time is hard. You may think your parents are mean or that you have a better way to do things. Sometimes you just aren't in the mood to do what they ask. But when you obey the first time they ask you to do something, it not only makes them happy, it makes *you* feel great! Most important, it pleases God. So get up and obey quickly. You'll be glad you did.

Lord,
I don't think I can obey my parents every time. I need Your help to do it. Will You please help me? Thank You.

Always Faithful

Even if we are not faithful, he will remain faithful.
He must be true to himself.

2 Timothy 2:13 NIrV

Have you ever meant to do the right thing but then didn't? Maybe you broke a promise or told a lie when you knew you shouldn't. Or watched a show you were told not to watch. How did you feel afterward?

We all do the wrong thing sometimes. Even grown-ups do. But the good news is that God loves us anyway. It doesn't matter how many times we mess up, God still wants us to climb up in His lap and snuggle. While we're there, it's good to tell Him we're sorry. He won't ever try to make us feel worse about what we did. Why? Because even when we make mistakes, God is always faithful. His love for us will never change. That's just the way He is. He can't be any different. If He could, then He wouldn't be God. He has to be true to who He is.

So the next time you mess up, remember God's waiting to hold you and show you just how much He loves you. Run to Him! He's always faithful.

God,

I can't believe how much You love me, but I'm glad You do. Help me to tell You I'm sorry when I need to and to do better the next time.

Absolutely, Positively

That should make you feel like saying, "The Lord helps me!
Why should I be afraid of what people can do to me?"
HEBREWS 13:6 CEV

What's something you feel really sure about—something that you know is absolutely, positively true?

Here's something else you can be sure of: "The Lord helps me! Why should I be afraid of what people can do to me?" The Bible says you can feel absolutely, positively sure of that. God *will* help you.

Imagine that mean kids are bothering you. How do you feel? Scared Like running away? Mad? Now imagine that your mighty, powerful God comes and stands behind you. He towers over you and the mean kids. He doesn't say anything but stares at the bullies. You look up at Him and He winks at you and smiles. You've got God on your side! Compared to God, the mean kids suddenly look small. They can't do anything to you! To your surprise, they run away in fear.

We can't really see God, but He's there, and He's just as real as your best friend. He was there for David when he faced the giant Goliath, and He'll be there for you, too. Absolutely, positively!

God,

thanks for being on my side. I know I can trust You to help me whenever I need it. Help me not to be afraid.

Good Faith

You should try very hard to add goodness to your faith.

2 PETER 1:5 NIrV

What is faith? Hebrews 11:1 says, "Faith is being sure of what we hope for. It is being certain of what we do not see" (NIrV). We can't see God, but we're sure He's real. We have the great hope that God the Father will send Jesus back to the earth so we can live together forever. If you believe those things, even though you can't see them and don't know when they will happen, then you have faith!

Our verse today says we should add goodness to our faith. We can do that by being kind and helpful, even when we don't feel like it. It's a funny thing, but when you do the right thing, you'll always be glad you did, even when you'd rather do something else. Adding goodness to your faith makes waiting for Jesus to come back a lot easier. Our time is spent thinking of others instead of ourselves. And that's a good feeling!

Think of a way you can help someone. Then do it! You'll be adding goodness to your faith, and that makes your faith stronger.

God, please help me to have a great big faith with lots of goodness mixed in. I believe in You.

Truth Telling

But God is faithful and fair. If we admit that we have sinned, he will forgive us our sins. He will forgive every wrong thing we have done. He will make us pure.

1 JOHN 1:9 NIrV

Have you ever broken something that your parents said not to touch? Did you tell them what happened right away, or did you wait until they found the broken pieces?

It's scary to admit when you've done something wrong. You might get in trouble. Your parents might get mad. Even if you don't tell, there's that icky feeling inside, knowing you're keeping a bad secret.

I've got good news for you! God never gets mad when you come to Him and tell Him you did something wrong. He may feel sad that you made a bad choice, but He's always glad you told Him. He wants to forgive you and help you try to do better next time. Some unhappy things may still happen because you sinned, but that's only God helping you learn not to do it again. He's always fair, no matter what. He wants to help you be clean and pure inside.

And guess what? Your parents feel the same way. They'd rather have you tell them when you do something wrong than find out later on their own. So take a deep breath and tell them the truth. God will help you.

Lord,

I want to be pure. Help me to be brave enough to tell my parents the truth when I do something wrong. Thank You for loving me.

"...as White as Snow."

His head and his hair were white like wool, as white as snow.
And his eyes were bright like flames of fire.

REVELATION 1:14 NLT

No one today really knows what Jesus looked like. But one old man described him in the Bible. John, who lived on a little island called Patmos about sixty-five years after Jesus died, had a vision of the Lord. He saw the resurrected Jesus.

John was praying on a Sunday when he heard a voice behind him—it turned out to be Jesus Christ. John wrote that Jesus was wearing a long robe with a gold sash across His chest. His hair was woolly, as white as snow. His eyes flashed like fire. His feet were like pure, shining bronze. His voice thundered like ocean waves that break on the shore. Seven stars were in His right hand, and a sharp sword came out of His mouth. His face was as bright as the sun on a perfectly clear day.

When John saw Jesus, he fainted. But Jesus said, "Don't be afraid! I am the first, the last, and the living one. I was dead, and look, I'm alive forever and ever!"

Think of that! Jesus is alive right now. He is holding and loving us like those seven bright stars in His hand.

Dear God,
thank You for being our wonderful and living Lord!

"...a New Heaven and a New Earth."

Then I saw a new heaven and a new earth. ....
And I saw the holy city, the new Jerusalem,
coming down from God out of heaven.

REVELATION 21:1–2 NLT

Do you know how the Bible ends? In the end, heaven comes to earth. John saw this in his vision. It is a holy city named the New Jerusalem. It will come down out of heaven from God. This city is like a beautiful bride who is ready to marry her husband.

John heard a voice coming from God's throne. "Look," the voice said. "The home of God is now among people! He will live with them. They will be His people. God will be with them. All their tears will be wiped away. There will be no more death, sorrow, crying, or pain. The old world is gone forever."

Then the one sitting on the throne said, "Look, I am making everything new!"

This wonderful city of God is the hope of every Christian. We will all be there living with God on the new earth.
This is God's promise: "It is finished! I'm the Alpha and the Omega—the beginning and the end. I will freely give the thirsty people water from the spring of the water of life. I'll be their God and they'll be My children."

Dear God,
thank You for Your glory that lasts forever and ever!

"...a Tree of Life."

And the angel showed me a pure river with the water of life,
clear as crystal, flowing from the throne of God and of the
Lamb, coursing down the center of the main street.
On each side of the river grew a tree of life.

REVELATION 22:1–2 NLT

Do you remember the first two chapters of the Bible? They tell the story of God's creation of the heavens, the earth, and all things. Adam and Eve were there living in a perfect garden in Eden. There was a river and the Tree of Life. These two chapters of the Bible tell of God's paradise. God was everything to the people who lived there. They loved and lived by God, and God loved them. Together they walked through the garden in the cool of the day.

Do you remember the third chapter of the Bible? In it, the man and woman were tempted away from God. Suddenly paradise was gone. They were cut off from the tree of life and lost everything. Then the Bible begins to tell the story of how God brings men and women back to Himself—back to paradise. This story runs for 1,885 chapters of sixty-six books of the Bible, which contain 31,000 verses! Finally the Book of Life is opened, and hell and death are thrown into the lake of fire.

Then come the last two chapters of the Bible. Here again is paradise, which is watered by the river of life. Here again is the Tree of Life. Here we love and live with God forever!

Dear God,
thank You for all You have done, what You are doing, and what You will do!

The King

He shall be great, and shall be called the Son of the Highest:
and the Lord God shall give unto him the throne of his father
David: And he shall reign over the house of Jacob for ever;
and of his kingdom there shall be no end.

LUKE 1:32–33 KJV

Most kings inherit their crowns from their fathers. When a king is born, he is called a prince. Then, when he is old enough, he becomes the king, and he rules over his kingdom. When he dies, or perhaps when he is too old to be a good ruler, one of his sons will become the king. Sometimes, a king will lose his kingdom altogether. Perhaps there is a war, and another country steals his kingdom away. Or perhaps the people of his own kingdom decide they want a different king.

Jesus is a different kind of king, for His kingdom will never end. He is called the Prince of Peace, but He is also the King of Kings. He has always been the king, and He always will be.

He is a good and kind ruler. He will never die, so He will never have to pass His crown on to anyone else. And no matter who may try to take His kingdom from Him, they will never win. The kingdom of God will remain forever, and Jesus will always be its ruler.

Dear Father,

thank You for sending Jesus
to be a good and kind ruler.
I'm glad He is the king,
and that His kingdom
will last forever.

About the Authors

Renae Brumbaugh lives in Texas with two noisy children and two dogs. She's authored four books in Barbour's Camp Club Girls series.

Linda Carlblom loves writing children's fiction and speaking to women and kids. She's active in her local church in Tempe, Arizona.

Jane Landreth enjoys touching young lives with God's love. She and her husband, Jack, reside in the Ozarks.

Daniel Partner is a freelance writer and editor in Oregon who has worked on many Barbour projects over the years